INTERNET PIRACY

James D. Torr, *Book Editor*

Bruce Glassman, *Vice President*
Bonnie Szumski, *Publisher*
Helen Cothran, *Managing Editor*

GREENHAVEN PRESS
An imprint of Thomson Gale, a part of The Thomson Corporation

Detroit • New York • San Francisco • San Diego • New Haven, Conn.
Waterville, Maine • London • Munich

© 2005 Thomson Gale, a part of The Thomson Corporation.

Thomson and Star Logo are trademarks and Gale and Greenhaven Press are registered trademarks used herein under license.

For more information, contact
Greenhaven Press
27500 Drake Rd.
Farmington Hills, MI 48331-3535
Or you can visit our Internet site at http://www.gale.com

LIBRARY OF CONGRESS CATALOGING-IN-PUBLICATION DATA

Internet piracy / James D. Torr, book editor.
    p. cm. — (At issue)
Includes bibliographical references and index.
ISBN 0-7377-2328-9 (lib. : alk. paper) — ISBN 0-7377-2329-7 (pbk. : alk. paper)
    1. Copyright—Electronic information resources—United States. 2. Sound recordings—Pirated editions—United States. 3. Piracy (Copyright)—United States. 4. Electronic commerce—Corrupt practices. I. Torr, James D., 1974– .
II. At issue (San Diego, Calif.)
KF3024.C6I58 2005
346.7304'82—dc22   2004042524

Printed in the United States of America

Contents

Introduction

Piracy is a form of theft. Specifically, it refers to the unauthorized copying or use of intellectual property. Intellectual property is knowledge or expression that is owned by someone. There are three major types of intellectual property: 1) creative works, including music, written material, movies, and software, which are protected by copyright law; 2) inventions, which are protected by patent law; and 3) brand-name products, which are protected by trademarks. Many of the issues surrounding piracy have to do with the difference between intellectual property and physical property. A CD, for example, is a piece of physical property, but the songs on the CD are intellectual property. A customer in a record store can purchase a CD, but someone else still owns—or more precisely, has the copyright to—the songs on the CD.

Piracy is primarily a problem for the entertainment and software industries, and therefore piracy most often involves violations of copyright law. Copyright is a legal right that protects creative works from being reproduced, performed, or disseminated without permission of the copyright owner. Essentially, a copyright gives its owner the exclusive right to make copies of the material in question.

Physical piracy—the copying and illegal sale of hard-copy CDs, videotapes, and DVDs—costs the music industry over $4 billion a year worldwide and the movie industry more than $3.5 billion. These numbers do not factor in the growing (and difficult to measure) problem of Internet piracy, in which music and movies are transferred to digital format and copies are made of the resulting computer file. Journalist Charles C. Mann explains why Internet piracy has the potential to be vastly more damaging to copyright industries than does physical piracy:

> To make and distribute a dozen copies of a videotaped film requires at least two videocassette recorders, a dozen tapes, padded envelopes and postage, and considerable patience. And because the copies are tapes of tapes, the quality suffers. But if the film has been digitized into a computer file, it can be E-mailed to millions of people in minutes; because strings of zeroes and ones can be reproduced with absolute fidelity, the copies are perfect. And online pirates have no development costs—they don't even have to pay for paper or blank cassettes—so they don't really have a bottom line.

The problem of Internet piracy did not gain national attention until Napster gained an enormous following in 1999.

The original Napster, created by then–college student Shawn Fanning in May 1999, was an online music service that enabled users to trade digital music flies. Napster used a technology known as peer-to-peer (P2P) networking. P2P networking essentially enables users to link their computers to other computers all across the network. Each user linked to the Napster network was able to share his or her music files with all the other users on the network, and each user was in turn able to download a copy of any music file on almost any other computer in the network. Napster claimed to have over 20 million users in July 2000, all of them making copies of each others' music.

By that time, Napster had become the subject of a massive controversy over online file sharing. Part of Napster's appeal was intertwined with the novelty of digital music: Many technically inclined people enjoyed using computer programs to organize their music collections and also liked being able to "burn" their own CD mixes. But the truly unprecedented aspect of Napster was that it gave users convenient access to a seemingly unlimited selection of music—for *free.*

Many fans of Napster did not view downloading music as piracy; they argued that Napster was a tool for music sharing, not stealing. They also contended that Napster gave new exposure to independent musicians. A teenager quoted in a June 2000 *Newsweek* feature on Napster summed up the typical view: "People don't think it's anything bad. . . . Or think about it at all." Meanwhile, the creators of Napster claimed that they were not responsible for what users did with their software.

The music industry disagreed. "What Napster is doing threatens legitimate E-commerce models and is legally and morally wrong," said Hilary Rosen, then-president of the Recording Industry Association of America (RIAA), the trade group that represents the U.S. music industry. Several record labels filed suit against Napster in December 1999, and after months of hearings, Napster was eventually shut down in July 2001.

To the frustration of the music industry, other file-sharing services emerged to take Napster's place. Some never gained a wide following of users, while others, such as Scour, Grokster, Morpheus, and Audiogalaxy, were targeted by copyright-infringement lawsuits. In late 2003 one of the most popular file-sharing services was Kazaa.

Although Kazaa and other file-sharing services allow users to share movie files and software as well as music, the music industry has led the fight against online file sharing. The RIAA and other organizations representing the music industry blame online file sharing for the 26 percent fall in global CD sales that occurred between 1999 and 2003. Many factors, including a sluggish economy and a lack of exciting pop music releases may be responsible for the decline, but as reporters Kenneth Terrell and Seth Rosen note, "digital piracy undoubtedly plays a role."

Kazaa is owned by Sharman Networks, which is based on the South Pacific island of Vanuatu and is thus less bound by U.S. laws. Kazaa and other descendants of Napster also use much more decentralized P2P networks than did Napster and cannot be eliminated by shutting down a few servers, as was the case with Napster. Therefore the music industry has begun focusing on individual file sharers rather than the P2P networks they use. In April 2003, for example, the recording industry sued four university students in federal court, accusing them of making thousands of songs available online for illegal downloading over P2P networks. The RIAA took a much larger step in September 2003, when it filed lawsuits against hundreds of Kazaa users, threatening them with penalties of thousands of dollars per copyrighted work that was shared online. "We've been telling people for a long time that file sharing copyrighted music is illegal, that you are not anonymous when you do it, and that engaging in it can have real consequences," said RIAA president Cary Sherman. She added, "Nobody likes playing the heavy and having to resort to litigation, but when your product is being regularly stolen, there comes a time when you have to take appropriate action." The RIAA offered to drop the individual lawsuits if the accused signed affidavits promising to stop sharing copyrighted music online.

The RIAA was able to file these lawsuits because of a June 2003 court ruling that said that Internet service providers (ISPs) were legally obligated to reveal the names of alleged file sharers. However, in December 2003 the U.S. Court of Appeals for the District of Columbia Circuit overturned the earlier rulings, stating that ISPs are not legally obligated to reveal their customers' identities. The ruling does not making file sharing legal, but it seriously hinders the music industry's strategy of targeting individual file sharers.

Many critics of the music industry's hard-line stance against online file sharing have argued that record companies need to embrace digital music. Legal, online music stores such as iTunes—and a relaunched version of Napster—have begun selling songs for $0.99, and their success suggests that many people are willing to pay for the convenience these services offer. Digital music sales may therefore offer a partial fix for the music industry's woes.

However, despite the efforts to fight it and the alternatives that are being offered, online file sharing remains rampant. An estimated 2.6 billion music files are downloaded through P2P networks each month, and more than four hundred thousand movies are downloaded each day. These figures will probably rise as computers become more powerful and broadband Internet access becomes more widespread.

The growth of online file sharing demonstrates how new technologies pose a fundamental problem for copyright law. Computers and the Internet have made the transmission of information easier than ever before, but the entire copyright system depends on the ability of copyright holders to control the transmission of information—specifically, to control who has the ability to access and copy their work.

The most vehement defenders of online file sharing believe that since the Internet has revolutionized the way people access information (including intellectual property such as music or movies), the law should change as well. John Perry Barlow, a cofounder of the Electronic Frontier Foundation, has argued that "copyright's not about creation, which will happen anyway—it's about distribution."

Applying this view to online music sharing, some defenders of the practice argue that copyright law is not designed to protect musicians, for whom it costs relatively little to create songs, but instead to reward record companies, who make large investments in choosing to produce thousands of CDs. Record companies, according to this logic, benefit society by helping to distribute creators' work, and the law should enable them to make a profit in doing so. But, the argument goes, since the Internet has made transmitting information almost free and thus made CDs largely unnecessary as a means of distributing music, record companies are no longer necessary—and neither are the laws that make copying songs illegal.

The idea that the Internet has made (or will make) copyright law unnecessary is a radical one. But elements of this view frequently surface in the debate about online file sharing. For example, John Naughton, a columnist for the *Observer*, writes that the RIAA's stance that online music sharing is "stealing" is misleading:

> Pretending that intellectual property is the same as any other kind of property is deeply misleading. For while there is no gain to society from plundering other people's physical property, there is clearly a social benefit from the wide dissemination of intellectual property—i.e., ideas and their expressions.

In Naughton's view, online file sharing does not qualify as "piracy" at all:

> We have to remind legislators that intellectual property rights are a socially-conferred privilege rather than an inalienable right, that copying is not always evil (and in some cases is actually socially beneficial) and that there is a huge difference between wholesale 'piracy'—the mass-production and sale of illegal copies of protected works—and the file-sharing that most internet users go in for.

Although online file sharing debuted in 1999, lawmakers and copyright industries are just beginning to address the myriad questions the practice has generated. In *At Issue: Internet Piracy*, authors attempt to answer some of those questions.

1

Online Music Sharing Is Wrong

Music United for Strong Internet Copyright

Music United for Strong Internet Copyright (MUSIC) is a coalition of more than twenty trade organizations within the music industry. Its mission is to promote public awareness of the legal and moral issues surrounding online music sharing.

The explosion in the illegal copying of music is having a terrible effect on the music industry and everyone who works in it. Downloading copyrighted music off the Internet without permission from the copyright owner is theft, plain and simple. Several court decisions have ruled that the "sharing" of music files via peer-to-peer (P2P) networks is in fact a violation of copyright laws; the courts also decided that guilty individuals may be prosecuted on criminal charges or sued. In addition to being against the law, stealing music compromises the livelihood of musicians, songwriters, record store owners, and employees—basically everyone in the music industry.

More than 2.6 billion files are illegally downloaded per month. The explosion in illegal copying is affecting the entire music community. And contrary to what some people would tell you, it's having a very real and harmful impact on countless musicians, songwriters, and performers—virtually everyone, from recording engineers to record-store clerks, who dreams about making a living providing music to the public.

The unauthorized reproduction and distribution of copyrighted music is *just as illegal as shoplifting a CD*. Burning CD's from peer-to-peer networks like Kazaa, Morpheus or Gnutella is against the law. The rules are very simple. Unless you own the copyright, it's not yours to distribute. . . .

It's a criminal act

Copyright law protects the *value* of creative work. When you make illegal copies of someone's creative work, you are *stealing* and *breaking the law*.

Most likely, you've seen the FBI warning on a movie DVD or VHS cassette—well, the same applies, with equal force, to music. If you have been illegally reproducing or distributing copyrighted music, maybe you should give it a closer read.

> Federal law provides severe civil and criminal penalties for the unauthorized reproduction, distribution, rental or digital transmission of copyrighted sound recordings. (Title 17, United States Code, Sections 501 and 506). The FBI investigates allegations of criminal copyright infringement and violators will be prosecuted.

You won't find these messages on music you've downloaded illegally, but the full weight of the law applies just the same. . . .

What the law says and what it means. If you make unauthorized copies of copyrighted music recordings, you're stealing. You're breaking the law, and you could be held legally liable for thousands of dollars in damages.

That's pretty important information to have, considering how serious it would be if you were caught and prosecuted by the authorities or sued in civil court. It's even more important that you understand that when you illicitly make or distribute recordings, you are taking something of value from the owner without his or her permission.

If you make unauthorized copies of copyrighted music recordings, you're stealing.

You may find this surprising. After all, when you're on the Internet, digital information can seem to be as free as air. But the fact is that U.S. copyright law prohibits the unauthorized duplication, performance or distribution of a creative work.

That means you need the permission of the copyright holder before you copy and/or distribute a copyrighted music recording. . . .

Don't you have a better way to spend five years and $250,000?

Examples of easy ways you could violate the law:

- Somebody you don't even know e-mails you a copy of a copyrighted song and then you turn around and e-mail copies to all of your friends.
- You make an MP3 copy of a song because the CD you bought expressly permits you to do so. But then you put your MP3 copy on the Internet, using a file-sharing network, so that millions of other people can download it.
- Even if you don't illegally offer recordings to others, you join a file-sharing network and download unauthorized copies of all the copyrighted music you want for free from the computers of other network members.
- In order to gain access to copyrighted music on the computers of other network members, you pay a fee to join a file-sharing network that isn't authorized to distribute or make copies of copyrighted music. Then you download unauthorized copies of all the music you want.
- You transfer copyrighted music using an instant messenging service.

- You have a computer with a CD burner, which you use to burn copies of music you have downloaded onto writable CDs for all of your friends.

Do the crime, do the time

If you do not have legal permission, and you go ahead and copy or distribute copyrighted music anyway, you can be prosecuted in criminal court and/or sued for damages in civil court.

- Criminal penalties for first-time offenders can be as high as five years in prison and $250,000 in fines.
- Civil penalties can run into many thousands of dollars in damages and legal fees. The minimum penalty is $750 per song.

The "No Electronic Theft Law" (NET Act) is similar on copyright violations that involve digital recordings:

- Criminal penalties can run up to 5 years in prison and/or $250,000 in fines, even if you didn't do it for monetary or financial or commercial gain.
- If you did expect something in return, even if it just involves swapping your files for someone else's, as in MP3 trading, you can be sentenced to as much as 5 years in prison.
- Regardless of whether you expected to profit, you're still liable in civil court for damages and lost profits of the copyright holder.
- Or the copyright holders can sue you for up to $150,000 in statutory damages for each of their copyrighted works that you illegally copy or distribute.

If you make digital copies of copyrighted music on your computer available to anyone through the Internet without the permission of the copyright holder, you're stealing. And if you allow a P2P file-sharing network to use part of your computer's hard drive to store copyrighted recordings that anyone can access and download, you're on the wrong side of the law.

Having the hardware to make unauthorized music recordings doesn't give you the right to steal. Music has value for the artist and for everyone who works in the industry. Please respect that.

What the courts have ruled

What the courts have to say about illegal uploading and downloading . . . :

> As stated by Record Company Plaintiffs in their brief, "Aimster predicates its entire service upon furnishing a 'road map' for users to find, copy, and distribute copyrighted music.". . . We agree. Defendants [Aimster] manage to do everything but actually steal the music off the store shelf and hand it to Aimster's users.
> —*Aimster Copyright Litigation. 01-C-8933, MDL # 1425 (Memorandum Opinion and Order, September 4, 2002).*

> . . . they [Aimster] apparently believe that the ongoing, massive, and unauthorized distribution and copying of Record

Company Plaintiffs' copyrighted works by Aimster's end users somehow constitutes "personal use." This contention is specious and unsupported by the very case on which Defendants rely.

> *—Aimster Copyright Litigation. 01-C-8933, MDL # 1425 (Memorandum Opinion and Order, September 4, 2002).*

Napster users infringe at least two of the copyright holders' exclusive rights. . . .Napster users who upload file names to the search index for others to copy violate plaintiffs' distribution rights. Napster users who download files containing copyrighted music violate plaintiffs' reproduction rights. . . . [V]irtually all Napster users engage in the unauthorized downloading or uploading of copyrighted music. . . .

> *—A&M Records v. Napster, Inc., 239 F.3d 1004 (9th Cir. 2001).*

Although defendant [MP3.com] seeks to portray its service as the "functional equivalent" of storing its subscribers' CDs, in actuality defendant is re-playing for the subscribers converted versions of the recording it copied, without authorization, from plaintiffs' copyrighted CDs. On its face, this makes out a presumptive case of infringement under the Copyright Act. . . .

> *—UMG Recordings, Inc. v. MP3.com, Inc., 92 F. Supp. 2d 349 (S.D.N.Y. 2000). . . .*

What's OK and what's not

Technology has made digital copying easier than ever. But just because advances in technology make it possible to copy music doesn't mean it's legal to do so. Here are tips from some record labels on how to enjoy the music while respecting rights of others in the digital world. Stick with these, and you'll be doing right by the people who created the music.

Internet copying:

- It's okay to download music from sites authorized by the owners of the copyrighted music, whether or not such sites charge a fee.
- It's *never* okay to download unauthorized music from pirate sites (web or FTP) or peer-to-peer systems. Examples of peer-to-peer systems making unauthorized music available for download include: Kazaa, Grokster, Imesh, WinMX, LimeWire, Bearshare, Aimster, Morpheus, and Gnutella.
- It's *never* okay to make unauthorized copies of music available to others (that is, uploading music) on peer-to-peer systems.

Copying CDs:

- It's okay to copy music onto an analog cassette, but not for commercial purposes.
- It's also okay to copy music onto special Audio CD-R's, mini-discs, and digital tapes (because royalties have been paid on them)—but, again, not for commercial purposes.

- Beyond that, there's no legal "right" to copy the copyrighted music on a CD onto a CD-R. However, burning a copy of a CD onto a CD-R, or transferring a copy onto your computer hard drive or your portable music player, won't usually raise concerns so long as:
  - The copy is made from an authorized original CD that you legitimately own.
  - The copy is just for your personal use. *It's not a personal use—in fact, it's illegal—to give away the copy or lend it to others for copying.*
- The owners of copyrighted music have the right to use protection technology to allow or prevent copying.
- Remember, it's never okay to sell or make commercial use of a copy that you make.

Are there occasionally exceptions to these rules? Sure. A "garage" or unsigned band might *want* you to download its own music; but, bands that own their own music are free to make it available legally by licensing it. And, remember that there are lots of authorized sites where music can be downloaded for free. Better to be safe than sorry—don't assume that downloading or burning is legal just because technology makes it easy to do so. . . .

The victims of "free" music

A lot of people who copy and distribute music illegally try to rationalize their behavior by arguing that the people who make recordings are all rich anyway, and that music should be free.

To assert that music should be free is the same as saying it has no value—that music is worthless. It's not. Music doesn't just happen. It's made, note by note, beat by beat, by people who work hard to get it right.

For the artist, the hard work requires not only a major emotional and intellectual commitment, but also long hours, intense concentration, and real financial risk. We like to talk about the imagination, soul, and courage involved in creative work. But making music is also about career and financial well-being. It's about putting food on the table and covering the rent. It's about making enough money to pay for all that equipment and rehearsal time, about keeping yourself afloat as you strive to succeed in a highly competitive industry.

What gives the music value is not only that you like it, but also that you buy it. If you steal it, you're not just stealing from a record company. You're stealing from the very artists you love and admire.

Most of us would never even consider stealing something of value from a neighbor's house. Our conscience, our sense of right and wrong, keep us from doing it. Sure, we know there are criminal penalties, but the main reason we don't steal is because we know it's wrong. . . .

The harm to musicians and other music industry employees

Another rationalization for stealing music is that illegal copying is a victimless crime that really doesn't hurt anyone.

Tell that to the struggling young musicians in a garage band who can't get signed because record sales are down.

Or tell it to the young singer-songwriter whose career dead-ends because people would rather download her music for free.

There's no question that Internet exposure can be a great thing for new artists. For many up-and-coming bands, there's no better way of getting noticed and establishing a following than creating a website and putting your stuff out there for the online world to hear. But there's a difference between checking out a band that chooses to let people download its music for free and deciding for yourself that somebody's new music should be spread all over the Internet.

Just because advances in technology make it possible to copy music doesn't mean it's legal to do so.

Making records is an expensive undertaking. So is building a career. If people aren't willing to pay for the music they love, the record companies will find it increasingly difficult to commit the kind of resources it takes to discover and develop new talent.

Songwriters and artists, whether established or up-and-coming, aren't the only people hurt by illegal copying. In the U.S. alone, the music industry employs some 50,000 people—and very few of them are rich rock stars.

Stealing music also threatens the livelihoods of the thousands of technicians, CD-plant workers, warehousemen, and other non-musicians who are employed in the music business helping to create and deliver the music you love.

2

The Harms of Online Music Sharing Are Exaggerated

Orson Scott Card

Orson Scott Card is the author of more than thirty novels and a regular contributor to the Ornery American, *an online political newspaper.*

The music industry has greatly exaggerated both the threat that online file sharing poses and the harm that it has caused. CD sales are not down just because of file sharing, but also because today's music offerings are poor and because most people have by now upgraded their music collections from vinyl LPs and cassette tapes to CDs. Moreover, music on the Internet generally helps artists get more exposure—it just may not help record companies sell more CDs. What the online music sharing controversy has shown is that copyright laws should be updated to better benefit both artists and consumers. Record companies should stop pretending to be victims, stop treating their customers as criminals, and start working on adapting their business models to fit with current technology.

S ince every penny I earn depends on copyright protection, I'm all in favor of reasonable laws to do the job.

But there's something kind of sad about the recording industry's indecent passion to punish the "criminals" who are violating their rights.

Copyright is a temporary monopoly granted by the government—it creates the legal fiction that a piece of writing or composing (or, as technologies were created, a recorded performance) is property and can only be sold by those who have been licensed to do so by the copyright holder.

Without copyright, once a work was performed or printed, other people who saw or heard or read it could simply do their own performance or print their own editions, and keep all the money without paying a dime to the creator of the work.

At the same time, a book or song isn't land or even corporate stock. In exchange for the private monopoly of copyright, when it expires the work is then free for anyone to perform or print or record.

Until 1978, copyright only lasted 52 years in the U.S.—and then only if you remembered to renew it. There were other technical lapses that could result in the inadvertent loss of copyright—it wasn't really user-friendly.

And the most obnoxious feature of the law was that some authors outlived their copyright. Their most popular works would go into public domain while they were still alive and counting on the income. It's like revoking someone's Social Security at age 72, just because they had the temerity not to die when demographics predicted they would.

Since 1978, the law was changed so that copyright lasted until a certain number of years after the author's death. So not only did the author never outlive the copyright, but the author's dependents could continue to derive income from it for some time.

The entire music business absolutely depends on the social interaction of kids to make hits.

Also, copyright began, not when the work was listed with the Library of Congress, but rather from the moment of creation.

But there were loopholes. If you wrote something as an employee of a company that paid you a salary for creating it, then your writing was a "work made for hire" and the copyright belonged to the company. You had no rights.

Here's where the ugly stuff begins. A lot of publishers began routinely requiring writers to sign contracts that declared that what they wrote was a "work for hire," so that the authors wouldn't own any part of their own work. Of course the companies didn't actually hire the writers and give them benefits, like real employees. It was basically highway robbery—the companies demanded that either the writers sign their names to a lie and give up all their rights, or the company wouldn't publish it.

Only a few of us were stubborn enough to refuse to sign work for hire contracts. It was an expensive moral quibble, but I have real objections to perjuring myself and pretending that I was hired by a company when in fact I never was. If I took all the risks and wrote something on spec, then the copyright should belong to me. I'd license them to do whatever was needed, but I wouldn't, in effect, declare *them* to be the author of *my* work.

Who are the thieves in this house?

So it's pretty hilarious to hear record company executives and movie studio executives get all righteous about copyright. They've been manipulating copyright laws for years, and all the manipulations were designed to steal everything they could from the actual creators of the work.

Do you think these companies care about the money that the actual creators of the work are being deprived of when people copy CDs and DVDs?

Here's a clue: Movie studios have, for decades, used "creative accounting" to make it so that even hit movies never manage to break even, thus depriving the creative people of their "percentage of profits." A few have dared to sue, but most figure that it isn't worth the ill will. (The sentence "You'll never work in this town again" runs through their minds. They remember what happened to [1940s actor] Cliff Robertson after he blew the whistle on an executive who was flat-out embezzling!)

And record companies manage to skim enormous amounts of money from every CD sold. As you can easily calculate by going to the computer store and figuring out the price of an individual recordable blank CD. Figure that the record companies have been paying a fraction of *that* price for years. Then subtract that from the price of a CD. Figure the songwriters and performers are getting some ludicrously small percentage—less than twenty percent, I'd bet—and all the rest flows to the record company.

In other words, the people complaining about all the internet "thieves" are, by any reasonable measure, rapacious profiteers who have been parasitically sucking the blood out of copyrights on other people's work.

And I say this with the best will in the world. In fact, these companies have expenses. There are salaries to pay. Some of the salaries are earned.

But remember that huge fortunes like, say, David Geffen's were made by getting ownership of record publishing companies. Count on it—Geffen got a lot richer than any but a handful of the actual performers. And when their careers are over, the record company owner keeps right on earning.

Not only that, but the digital technologies that allow perfect-quality copying came as a huge windfall to the studios and record companies.

Most of the people who are getting those free MP3s would not be buying the CDs anyway.

I basically replaced all my vinyl records and cassette tapes with CDs, and then replaced all our VHS tapes and laserdiscs with DVDs. The record companies and studios would have laughed if somebody said, "This is just an upgrade. I should be able to turn in my vinyl and cassettes for CDs and my videotapes for DVDs, for no more than the actual cost of production." Ha ha ha ha ha.

In all the ridiculously overblown "estimates" of how much the studios and record companies are "losing" from "piracy," nobody bothers to calculate just how much extra money they made from consumers paying full price for music and movies they had already paid full price for only a few years before.

That's all right, you see, because that helps the companies' bottom line, whereas piracy hurts it.

But how much?

The hit-making machine

The real pirates—people who make knock-off copies of CDs and DVDs and sell them in direct competition (or in foreign markets)—make a lot of money in some markets, but most of those are overseas. It's a problem, but some reasonable combination of private investigation and police work and international treaties should deal with that.

Internet "pirates," though, usually are more like a long-distance group that trades CDs around.

If you got together with a few of your neighbors and each of you bought different CDs and then lent them to each other, that wouldn't even violate copyright.

In fact, the entire music business absolutely depends on the social interaction of kids to make hits. You stop kids from sharing music, and you've shut down the hit-making machine.

The record companies pretend they're protecting the rights of the musicians, but you have to be deeply dumb to believe that.

Copyright violation comes from the fact that digital copies—even the compressed MP3 format—are nearly perfect. And when you "lend" your copy to someone over the internet, you still have your original. And he can lend to ten more or a hundred more or a thousand more, and the record company is only paid for that first copy.

Well, that's not a good thing—if that became the primary way music was published.

The record companies swear that it's making a serious inroad on sales, and they can prove it. How? By showing that their sales are way down in the past few years.

It couldn't possibly be because (a) most of us have already replaced all our old vinyl and cassettes, so all that windfall money is no longer flowing in, or (b) because the record companies have made some really lousy decisions as they tried to guess what we consumers would want to buy.

It couldn't possibly be that they've targeted all their marketing at precisely the market segment—high school and college students—who are most likely to be sharing MP3s over the internet.

Maybe if they started marketing more music that people my age would enjoy, they'd find that, lo and behold, there *are* customers who prefer to buy music the legal way!

It has all happened before

The irony is that we've played out this whole scenario before, more than once. When radio first started broadcasting records instead of live performances, the music publishing industry became livid. This was going to hurt sales! A compromise was reached whereby radio stations paid small fees to the publishers for each playing of a record.

But the truth is that it's a lot of bother for nothing. Radio didn't hurt record sales. Radio *made* record sales, because people wanted to own the records they heard on the radio. Radio let people hear musicians they might never have found otherwise.

Same thing with TV and movies. Yes, TV wiped out the B-movie market segment and it killed newsreels—but it opened up a lucrative aftermarket that kept movies alive long after they would have stopped earning money. That's how *Wizard of Oz* and *It's a Wonderful Life* and many other movies became American icons.

And again, with the VCR, studios were terrified that people would tape things off the air and stop paying money for movies. (And the TV networks were terrified that people would tape shows and skip over the ads; they didn't realize that most of us are too lazy to skip over commercials.)

And rental videotapes! That was the end of the world!

When the studios finally stopped charging ninety bucks for a videotape, they discovered that the videotape (and now DVD) aftermarket was often bigger than the original theatrical release.

The internet is similar, but not identical, to these situations.

First, most of the people who are getting those free MP3s would not be buying the CDs anyway. They're doing this in order to get far more music than they can actually afford. That means that if they weren't sharing MP3s online, they would simply have less music—or share CDs hand to hand. It does *not* mean that they would have bought CDs to get the tunes they're downloading from Napster-like sharing schemes.

That's why I laugh at their estimates of "lost sales."

How to teach your customers to hate you

It only gets stupider the more you think about it. The kids they're trying to prosecute and punish are in exactly the demographic that advertisers are most eager to target, not because they have the most money—far from it, people *my* age have all the money—but because they're "brandable." They haven't yet committed themselves to brand loyalty. They're open to all kinds of possibilities. And advertisers want to get to them and imprint their brands so that they'll own these consumers as they get older and start earning money.

So just how smart is it to indelibly imprint on their young minds a link between your corporate brand and outrageous punishments for music sharing?

Let's keep this in perspective. We're not talking about murder here, or child molestation, or even speeding on the highway. No one's life is put at risk. In all likelihood, nobody is really losing any money they would have had anyway. So just what kind of punishment is really deserved?

There is such a thing as defeating your own purpose. Like Queen Mary I of England who tried to restore Catholic fidelity by burning a couple of hundred Protestants whose sins were as trivial as buying a Bible and having people read it to you. Every burning made it more certain that Catholicism would become loathsome to more and more of the population.

I was especially amused at Utah Senator Orrin Hatch's support for seeding the MP3-sharing sites with computer-destroying viruses.

I mean, this is one of the leading figures on the Senate Judiciary Committee, and he actually wanted to punish people without any kind of due process—and all for an offense against copyright.

Open sharing of music files doesn't actually hurt the creators of music. It helps them. When friends can say, "Have you heard Eva Cassidy's music? Here, I'll send you a couple of songs, you won't believe how good she is," that's called "word of mouth," and what you'll get is more and more people who attend her live performances and buy her CDs.

More sales for musicians that might otherwise never have been heard of.

You should hear singers like Janis Ian go on about how much *good* file-sharing does for the careers of musicians who aren't the pets of the record companies. The record companies pretend they're protecting the rights of the musicians, but you have to be deeply dumb to believe that. What they mean is that they want to protect the rights of the musicians they have under contract—even if their "protection" hurts everybody else.

The real gripe for the record companies is not these fictional "lost sales." What's keeping them up at night is the realization that musicians don't need record companies any more.

Musicians can go into a studio, record their own music exactly as they want it, and not as some executive says they have to record it because "that's what the kids want."

Then they can sell CDs at their live performances and set up online, with a bunch of MP3s that people can share around. They also can sell CDs, and without a lot of expensive record company overhead.

Of course, fulfilment and website management can be an expensive pain, so what will emerge is a new kind of recording company—full-service online stores that make only as many copies of a CD as are ordered, so there's no inventory to maintain. They'll take a much smaller share of the money than the existing companies do, so the CDs can sell for much less—while the artist still makes more money per sale than the big record companies ever allowed.

Change the law to help the artists

Meanwhile, let's remember that the studios and record companies have recently been manipulating the copyright laws to their own—not the artists'—advantage.

When a corporation is listed as the "author" of a copyrighted work, then what does lifetime-plus-twenty or lifetime-plus-fifty really mean? Whose lifetime?

And extending copyright to ludicrous lengths of time is against the public interest. Twenty years after the author's death *or* the author's hundredth birthday, whichever comes last—that's a workable standard to provide for the author and his or her immediate heirs. It comes to an end, and the work enters the public domain as it should.

[Record] companies . . . have become bloated on windfall profits and ruthless exploitation of other people's talents [and] are now terrified that the gravy train will go away.

And let's eliminate this nonsense about corporate authorship. If a corporation claims to be the "author" for copyright purposes, then the whole life of the copyright should be twenty years, period. Corporations aren't authors of anything, ever, and they don't deserve the protections actual human beings have. They make most of their money in twenty years, except on a handful of works that enter the public consciousness. But just like trademarks that become ordinary words, like aspirin, it is precisely in these cases that corporately-authored works should enter the public domain quickly.

If you changed the law that way, suddenly "work for hire" contracts would disappear, and the real creators would be treated with more respect by the big companies—because they'd much rather have a fair contract with an author whose copyright will last many decades than to have outright "authorship" of a twenty-year copyright.

The companies would even have a vested interest in helping creative people live longer. Instead of trying to give them ulcers, heart attacks, strokes, fatal depressions, and reasons to drink.

How to stop the file-sharing

Truth to tell, I don't have much patience with the websites and systems that allow indiscriminate sharing of MP3s among strangers. I'd like to see them shut down. But they can't be, not without changing international agreements, because how can the U.S. government stop a file-sharing scheme that works on a server in Singapore? And Orrin Hatch's killer-virus scheme would be a form of international terrorism.

The same thing that keeps us from blocking the scourge of internet porn also keeps us from being able to take any practical measures to block MP3-sharing websites. And frankly, I think the porn sites cause far more harm to Americans than MP3-sharing. If the government goes after teen-agers sharing songs but does nothing about family-wrecking, soul-numbing porn, then something is deeply, deeply wrong.

Do you know how to stop file-sharing on anything other than a friend-to-friend, word-of-mouth basis?

Instead of turning the file-sharers into martyred heroes, the way the short-sighted executives want to do, just educate people that it's OK to let people hear a sample, but don't give away whole albums of work you didn't create. This is not a hard concept; people would get it.

Scorn works far better than lawsuits and punitive damages at changing society. I already react that way when somebody says, "Let me copy the CD for you." I affix them with a steely glare and say, "Do you own the copyright for that?" They usually say something face-saving, and I let them, because I'm not a puritan about it. But they not only never offer to copy songs for *me*, most of them also get more nervous to offer it to other people.

That will stamp out the "sharing" of whole CDs pretty quickly, if it catches on.

The same technique is the only effective one against the social spread of hard drugs. Most people only try self-destructive drugs because they think their peers will think they're cool for doing it. If their peers treated it with the same scorn they now offer those who, say, attend Sunday school, how many people would use drugs?

Do you think the use of cocaine would have become so widespread if it hadn't been treated as "cool" by the very studio and record company executives who are now in favor of rigid copyright law enforcement?

Fair is fair. I think any company that ever had an employee provide illegal drugs for musicians, or for anyone else at a company function, should be declared to have no standing to bring suit against anybody for copyright law infringement. The drugs they knowingly passed around (and, I would guess, still continue to pass around, if more discreetly) have killed far more people than Napster ever would have. There ought to be a hypocrisy penalty.

Strip away all the pretension, and what you really have is this: Rapacious companies that have become bloated on windfall profits and ruthless exploitation of other people's talents are now terrified that the gravy train will go away.

Because in the brave new world of online distribution of cheap CDs, do you know who the *only* losers would be? Big-salary executives and owners of big record companies.

The movie studio executives are safer—it takes big money to make big movies, and nobody can distribute on the net the experience of going into a theater to see a first-run movie.

Clean up your own act first

Americans are generally good people. If you explain to them *why* a rule is necessary, they'll generally go along with it.

But you have to get rid of the hypocrisy first. File-sharing is not the end of the world, and the existence of music and movies are not being threatened, any more than they were with the advent of radio, television, and VCRs.

And let's just laugh at the self-righteousness of the "injured" studios and record companies. We can't take them seriously until they've tried the obvious *market* responses:

Drop those CD prices to a reasonable level—even if it means firing some of those big-salary execs and cutting out some of the percs. (It won't take the record companies long to figure out how to take a percentage of concert performances to make up for lost income, anyway—or are they already doing it?)

Start treating the artists better, and let copyright be awarded to the creators, not the backers. When the audience sees that copyright law is protecting the musicians from the corporate exploiters, then they'll be more likely to obey the copyright law. The emotional connection is between musician and audience.

Which is why the companies should stop threatening us and our children with ludicrous prosecution, or with software designed to sabotage our right to make backup copies and transfer files from one player to another for our legitimate personal use.

The more visible you make yourselves, all you executives, the more everybody will hate you. Disappear from the public eye and revise your business model to fit the current technology.

Meanwhile, any copy-protection scheme you come up with that would make it harder for me to copy songs onto the player I use when I'm running, and I'll simply stop buying any music from your company. I already have a lot of music. I can listen to it for years before I need to buy another CD, if you've made it so I can't use it in the lawful ways that I want to.

Then let's get back to the real world, instead of wasting any more time on the petty and mostly self-inflicted problems of rich but badly-managed corporations.

3

Many People Do Not View Online Music Sharing as Wrong

Anthony G. Gorry

Anthony G. Gorry is a professor of management and computer science at Rice University.

The music industry is understandably upset at the rampant, unauthorized sharing of music files via the Internet, and has begun filing lawsuits against individuals who engage in the activity. The music industry may view online music sharing as piracy, but many people—particularly youth, who make up the majority of file sharers—do not see the issue in such black-and-white terms. While young people do not generally condone stealing, many of them point out that making a copy of copyrighted property is not exactly the same as stealing a piece of physical property such as a book. If the music industry is to prosper, it must recognize that technology has changed the way that people view music rather than condemning all file-sharers as criminals.

Sometimes when my students don't see life the way I do, I recall the complaint from *Bye Bye Birdie*, "What's the matter with kids today?" Then I remember that the "kids" in my class are children of the information age. In large part, technology has made them what they are, shaping their world and what they know. For my students, the advance of technology is expected, but for me, it remains both remarkable and somewhat unsettling.

In one course I teach, the students and I explore the effects of information technology on society. Our different perspectives on technology lead to engaging and challenging discussions that reveal some of the ways in which technology is shaping the attitudes of young people. An example is our discussion of intellectual property in the information age, of crucial importance to the entertainment business.

Anthony G. Gorry, "Steal This MP3 File," *Chronicle of Higher Education*, vol. 49, May 23, 2003.

In recent years, many users of the Internet have launched an assault on the music business. Armed with tools for "ripping" music from compact discs and setting it "free" in cyberspace, they can disseminate online countless copies of a digitally encoded song. Music companies, along with some artists, have tried to stop this perceived pillaging of intellectual property by legal and technical means. The industry has had some success with legal actions against companies that provide the infrastructure for file sharing, but enthusiasm for sharing music is growing, and new file-sharing services continue to appear.

The Recording Industry Association of America recently filed lawsuits against four college students, seeking huge damages for "an emporium of music piracy" run on campus networks. However, the industry settled those lawsuits less than a week after a federal judge in California ruled against the association in another case, affirming that two of the Internet's most popular music-swapping services are not responsible for copyright infringements by their users. (In the settlement, the students admitted no wrongdoing but agreed to pay amounts ranging from $12,000 to $17,500 in annual installments over several years and to shut down their file-sharing systems.)

With so many Internet users currently sharing music, legal maneuvers alone seem unlikely to protect the industry's way of doing business. Therefore, the music industry has turned to the technology itself, seeking to create media that cannot be copied or can be copied only in prescribed circumstances. Finding the right technology for such a defense, however, is not easy. Defensive technology must not prevent legitimate uses of the media by customers, yet it must somehow ward off attacks by those seeking to "liberate" the content to the Internet. And each announcement of a defensive technology spurs development of means to circumvent it.

In apparent frustration, some companies have introduced defective copies of their music into the file-sharing environment of the Internet, hoping to discourage widespread downloading of music. But so far, the industry's multifaceted defense has failed. Sales of CD's continue to decline. And now video ripping and sharing is emerging on the Internet, threatening to upset another industry in the same way.

Music companies might have more success if they focused on the users instead of the courts and technology. When they characterize file sharing as theft, they overlook the interplay of technology and behavior that has altered the very idea of theft, at least among young people. I got a clear demonstration of that change in a class discussion that began with the matter of a stolen book.

Is copying the same as stealing?

During the '60s, I was a graduate student at a university where student activism had raised tensions on and around the campus. In the midst of debates, demonstrations, and protests, a football player was caught leaving the campus store with a book he had not bought. Because he was well known, his misadventure made the school newspaper. What seemed to be a simple case of theft, however, took on greater significance. A number of groups with little connection to athletics rose to his defense, claiming that he had been entrapped: The university required that he have the book, the publisher charged an unfairly high price, and the bookstore put the book right in front of him, tempting him to steal it. So who could blame him?

Well, my students could. They thought it was clear that he had stolen the book. But an MP3 file played from my laptop evoked a different response. Had I stolen the song? Not really, because a student had given me the file as a gift. Well, was that file stolen property? Was it like the book stolen from the campus bookstore so many years ago? No again, because it was a copy, not the original, which presumably was with the student. But then what should we make of the typical admonition on compact-disc covers that unauthorized duplication is illegal? Surely the MP3 file was a duplication of the original. To what extent is copying stealing?

Treating customers like thieves is a certain recipe for failure.

The readings for the class amply demonstrated the complexity of the legal, technical, and economic issues surrounding intellectual property in the information age and gave the students much to talk about. Some students argued that existing regulations are simply inadequate at a time when all information "wants to be free" and when liberating technology is at hand. Others pointed to differences in the economics of the music and book businesses. In the end, the students who saw theft in the removal of the book back in the '60s did not see stealing in the unauthorized copying of music. For me, that was the most memorable aspect of the class because it illustrates how technology affects what we take to be moral behavior.

The technology of copying is closely related to the idea of theft. For example, my students would not take books from a store, but they do not consider photocopying a few pages of a book to be theft. They would not copy an entire book, however, perhaps because they vaguely acknowledge intellectual-property rights but probably more because copying would be cumbersome and time-consuming. They would buy the book instead. In that case, the very awkwardness of the copying aligns their actions with moral guidelines and legal standards.

But in the case of digital music, where the material is disconnected from the physical moorings of conventional stores and copying is so easy, many of my students see matters differently. They freely copy and share music. And they copy and share software, even though such copying is often illegal. If their books were digital and thus could be copied with comparable ease, they most likely would copy and share them.

Of course, the Digital Millennium Copyright Act, along with other laws, prohibits such copying. So we could just say that theft is theft, and complain with the song, "Why can't they be like we were, perfect in every way? . . . Oh, what's the matter with kids today?" But had we had the same digital technology when we were young, we probably would have engaged in the same copying and sharing of software, digital music, and video that are so common among students today. We should not confuse lack of tools with righteousness.

Technology has changed people's views

The music industry would be foolish to put its faith in new protective schemes and devices alone. Protective technology cannot undo the changes that previous technology has caused. Should the industry aggressively pursue legal defenses like the suits against the four college students? Such highly publicized actions may be legally sound and may even slow music sharing in certain settings, but they cannot stop the transformation of the music business. The technology of sharing is too widespread, and my students (and their younger siblings) no longer agree with the music companies about right and wrong. Even some of the companies with big stakes in recorded music seem to have recognized that lawsuits and technical defenses won't work. Sony, for example, sells computers with "ripping and burning" capabilities, MP3 players, and other devices that gain much of their appeal from music sharing. And the AOL part of AOL Time Warner is promoting its new broadband service for faster downloads, which many people will use to share music sold by the Warner part of the company.

The lesson from my classroom is that digital technology has unalterably changed the way a growing number of customers think about recorded music. If the music industry is to prosper, it must change, too—perhaps offering repositories of digital music for downloading (like Apple's newly announced iTunes Music Store), gaining revenue from the scope and quality of its holdings, and from a variety of new products and relationships, as yet largely undefined. Such a transformation will be excruciating for the industry, requiring the abandonment of previously profitable business practices with no certain prospect of success. So it is not surprising that the industry has responded aggressively, with strong legal actions, to the spread of file sharing. But by that response, the industry is risking its relationship with a vital segment of its market. Treating customers like thieves is a certain recipe for failure.

4

Internet Piracy Harms Artists

Phil Galdston

Phil Galdston is a professional songwriter. The following viewpoint is adapted from testimony that Galdston gave before Congress in September 2002.

Online music sharing and other illegal forms of copying music harm artists because they circumvent the intellectual property system through which artists get paid. The plight of songwriters illustrates this best: While musicians can earn a living by playing concerts, songwriters are only paid when people purchase the recorded versions of their songs (or pay a royalty fee to play them on the radio). Songwriters' intellectual copyrights on their work are their primary means of income, and Internet piracy is a serious and growing threat to this system of copyrights.

My name is Phil Galdston, and I am grateful for this opportunity to share some of my thoughts on musical intellectual property and the threat posed to the creators and owners of it. Just as importantly, I thank you for your willingness to examine issues crucial not only to songwriters and music publishers, but to music lovers across the nation and around the world. . . .

I am a composer, lyricist, and music publisher. I am not a recording artist (although once upon a time I was one). I am what is known as a pure songwriter—one who makes a living and supports his family by writing songs and submitting them to recording artists, producers, managers, labels, and anyone else who may help me get them recorded and exposed to the public.

For the record, although I do not speak on their behalf, you also should know that I am a long-time writer and publisher member of ASCAP (the American Society of Composers, Authors and Publishers) and a National Trustee and President of the New York Chapter of the National Academy of Recording Arts and Sciences, the group that bestows the GRAMMY© Awards.

Phil Galdston, testimony before the House Committee on the Judiciary, Washington, DC, September 26, 2002.

Over the course of my career, I have been fortunate enough to score hits on most of the major charts. Among my best known songs are: "Save the Best for Last" and "The Sweetest Days," which are among seven of my compositions recorded by Vanessa Williams; "Fly" and "The Last to Know," which are among five recorded by Celine Dion; "One Voice," which was recorded by Brandy, and was UNICEF's theme song in its 50th anniversary year; "World Without Love," which was a top ten record for the late country star, Eddie Rabbitt; and "It's Not Over (Til It's Over)," which was a top ten pop and rock hit for the rock band, Starship. My songs have appeared on more than 60 million records around the world, and I have been honored with a number of prestigious awards, including a Grammy nomination as Song of the Year and ASCAP's Song of the Year award.

Every time someone downloads a song of mine without authorization, I am losing . . . the ability to support my family . . . and the economic incentive to continue to create.

The hits and the awards aside, I am a songwriter and a small-business owner. My greatest achievement, and my greatest asset, is the catalogue of over 600 songs I have amassed in 37 years of writing. I am here today because that asset—my personal property—is under attack and is the subject of outright theft by those who obtain it without my permission and without compensating me. Please make no mistake about the situation songwriters face: our livelihoods are seriously and negatively impacted by unauthorized downloading of our work through peer-to-peer networks.

Real property vs. intellectual property

It would be nice to say that the business community in which we operate has developed a solution to this problem. But that is not the case, and, what's more, it may be extremely difficult to achieve in the short run. While there is little doubt in my mind that the solution to the crisis brought on by unauthorized downloading will be multi-faceted and will require a combination of effective digital rights management technologies, better online access to digital copyrighted material, better enforcement of copyright laws, and new technologies to aid in enforcement, at least part of the solution requires that our elected representatives help protect us.

To most people, the system compensating songwriters for the use of their copyrighted work is murky at best. I've noticed that most people who write or speak about it try to draw an analogy between intellectual property and so-called "real property." ("Downloading a song without the copyright owner's permission is like stealing a bicycle," and the like.) I've concluded that an appropriate analogy probably does not exist. And that tells me that what we songwriters create is rather unique.

Real property is comprised of raw materials that are produced by someone else. You just can't say that about songs. If I don't dream it up from my heart and my head, the song will not exist. The question most frequently asked of songwriters is "which comes first, the words or the music?" The answer is neither. What comes first is the inspiration, in all its wondrous variety of forms, none of which, or their final expression can be defined as "real property." Nonetheless, as you well know, it is property.

Rights to a song vs. rights to the recording of a song

To understand the position in which unauthorized downloading places songwriters, it is crucial to realize that, except in rather rare circumstances, we do not sell our songs. We license them to record companies, and other outlets, in return for royalties when and if they sell or are played in broadcast media. (For the purposes of this statement, I will use sales—or mechanical—royalties as my example. But the principles I will discuss apply to both mechanical and performance royalties.)

There is a given in the music community: "It all starts with the song." That is not only true of a great record or live performance, it's true of the rights that flow from a song's creation. And those underlying rights are separate and distinct from the rights attached to a recording of it. It is not just semantically incorrect to say that people download "record companies' songs." It is factually incorrect, as well. The record companies don't own the songs; they only own their recordings of those songs, not the songs. Songwriters—individual creators—own the songs.

All the angry talk about the major record companies, and their failings ("Why should I pay $18.00 for a CD with only one good song on it?" and the like) ignores this essential fact of ownership. A person who downloads a record of a song of mine without my permission may be trying to punish what they believe are big, bad record companies and greedy, selfish artists. But they're also punishing me, the person in the creative process who can least afford to be punished.

If anything, the current system already punishes me. When I license a song to a record company, I receive nothing—no fee, no advance, no payment of any kind. My compensation in that situation depends entirely on the success of the recording. If I am compensated, the already low rate is set by statute.

And frequently, labels demand that songwriters accept a three-quarter rate; six cents per copy sold instead of the current statutory rate of eight cents. (This is another situation I hope Congress will look into.) Please note that, while I may be paid less, I am never paid more. In fact, songwriters are the only people I know who are subject to a maximum wage.

What songwriters are losing

Although the law guarantees me compensation for every reproduction of my songs, including digital downloads, I do not receive anything for unauthorized downloads made through P2P [peer-to-peer] networks, like KaZaA, Morpheus, or Bear Share. If, as the most recent studies suggest, there are over three billion unauthorized downloads per month on all known peer-to-peer servers, well, you can do the math and see what songwriters are losing.

Therefore, while songwriters can see the value of the internet as a new and potentially vast source of revenue and exposure, while we want music internet services, including peer-to-peer services, to succeed, we must protect our right to be compensated for the use of our work. Every time someone downloads a song of mine without authorization, I am losing all that follows from it: the ability to support my family, the capital needed to continue to re-invest in my business, and the economic incentive to continue to create.

The right to grant or deny permission

In a peer-to-peer download, songwriters are losing something else: the right to grant or deny permission for that type of use. Of course, this is an essential aspect of ownership of any property. But in this case, it's a point illustrative of the complexity of the interlocking benefits of the use of songs. For example, although a good number of artists write the songs they record, their rights as recording artists and any artists royalties they may receive from the success of their recordings are entirely separate and distinct from those they enjoy as songwriters. By extension, my rights as a songwriter and any financial gain I may derive from the success of a recording made of it are distinct and separate from those of the artists who record my songs.

As a society, we are turning a blind eye to the theft of songs from the people who own them.

There are artists, labels, and artist-songwriters who may very well benefit from permitting audience members to download their work for free. Unlike pure songwriters, artists and labels have alternate sources of income and long-range goals to promote. Celine Dion or Brandy or Beyoncé Knowles may profit more from the sales of concert tickets or t-shirts than they lose from a free download promoting their merchandise. The artist and/or label may decide that it is more profitable to offer a free download in return for, say, an audience member's e-mail address. That trade provides them with an opportunity to market other products and services. Simply put, that is their choice; it should not be imposed on me. (By the way, I haven't seen a lot of "PHIL GALDSTON, PURE SONG-WRITER" t-shirts for sale.)

Songwriters are being punished for our success

It is sad to me that we songwriters are being punished for our success. The fact that it is difficult to go anywhere in "the civilized world" without constantly hearing songs—the vast majority of them written by American songwriters—is tribute to the immense popularity of our work. Be it a store, a mall, a movie theater, a living room with a TV on, a dorm room with a computer, a restaurant with a radio playing, or even the much-maligned dentist's office or elevator, the soundtrack to our lives is a stream of songs. And I imagine that, for many, this ubiquity, born of popularity, is the source of the misguided idea that, because music is in the air, it should or must be free. On the contrary, music is only in the air because my colleagues and I, through inspiration and hard work, have put it there.

All of this is about the basic principles of private property—principles that I have to believe most of those promoting or defending unauthorized peer-to-peer downloads would defend in any other situation. If all those offering illegal downloads would put as much effort into working with us (or, at least, obeying the law), we'd all have a system that was fair, legal, and entertaining.

How Congress can help

What can Congress do to help copyright owners coping with the damage and the continued threat from unauthorized downloads? I think the answer is simple and sensible: help us help ourselves.

We're probably most similar to the owners of satellites and cable systems, who face no liability when they use electronic countermeasures to stop the pirating of their signals and programming. However, at this point, due to the wide range of many anti-hacking laws, our legal ability to prevent the theft of our property through peer-to-peer systems is inhibited by a high degree of liability. . . .

I know that you can help us. I hope you are willing to do so. This is about much more than just compensation or permission; this is about the health of music. For, who will be drawn to a life creating music, if making music cannot provide a livelihood? This also is about respecting each other's property. My wife and I have taught our children that it is wrong to steal. Such unethical or immoral behavior, we instruct them, is never acceptable. And yet, as a society, we are turning a blind eye to the theft of songs from the people who own them.

Finally, music, along with our other powerful cultural expressions, is one of this country's leading exports and greatest ambassadors. If we turn our back on those who create it, what will we be saying to our composers and lyricists? To our children? What will we be saying to the rest of the world?

5

Online Music Sharing May Benefit Artists

Janis Ian

Janis Ian is a professional musician who has recorded more than fifteen albums.

There is little evidence that online music sharing is financially harming musicians, and plenty of evidence that it is benefiting them. The recording industry has objected to every new consumer recording technology—including VCRs and tape recorders—but each new technology has ultimately helped artists by enabling more people to hear their work. The Internet is similarly allowing more people to hear new and independent artists. The recording industry claims it is fighting online music to protect artists, but in reality it is fighting online music sharing in order to maintain its control over artists. Free exposure through online music sharing may not benefit major recording companies, but it does benefit artists, the public, and the music industry as a whole.

When I research an article, I normally send 30 or so emails to friends and acquaintances asking for opinions and anecdotes. I usually receive 10–20 in reply. But not so on this subject!

I sent 36 emails requesting opinions and facts on free music downloading from the Net. I stated that I planned to adopt the viewpoint of devil's advocate: free Internet downloads are good for the music industry and its artists.

I've received, to date, over 300 replies, every single one from someone legitimately "in the music business."

What's more interesting than the emails are the phone calls. I don't know anyone at NARAS [National Academy of Recording Arts and Sciences] (home of the Grammy Awards), and I know Hilary Rosen (former head of the Recording Industry Association of America, or RIAA) only vaguely. Yet within 24 hours of sending my original email, I'd received two messages from Rosen and four from NARAS requesting that I call to "discuss the article."

Huh. Didn't know I was that widely read.

Ms. Rosen, to be fair, stressed that she was only interested in presenting RIAA's side of the issue, and was kind enough to send me a fair amount of statistics and documentation, including a number of focus group studies RIAA had run on the matter.

However, the problem with focus groups is the same problem anthropologists have when studying peoples in the field—the moment the anthropologist's presence is known, everything changes. Hundreds of scientific studies have shown that any experimental group *wants to please the examiner.* For focus groups, this is particularly true. Coffee and donuts are the least of the pay-offs.

The NARAS people were a bit more pushy. They told me downloads were "destroying sales", "ruining the music industry", and "costing *you* money".

Costing *me* money? I don't pretend to be an expert on intellectual property law, but I do know one thing. If a music industry executive claims I should agree with their agenda because it will make me more money, I put my hand on my wallet . . . and check it after they leave, just to make sure nothing's missing.

Am I suspicious of all this hysteria? You bet. Do I think the issue has been badly handled? Absolutely. Am I concerned about losing friends, opportunities, my 10th Grammy nomination by publishing this article? Yeah. I am. But sometimes things are just *wrong*, and when they're *that* wrong, they have to be addressed.

Free downloads are good for artists

The premise of all this ballyhoo is that the industry (and its artists) are being harmed by free downloading.

Nonsense. Let's take it from my personal experience. My site (www.janisian.com) gets an average of 75,000 hits a year. Not bad for someone whose last hit record was in 1975. When Napster was running full-tilt, we received about 100 hits a month from people who'd downloaded *Society's Child* or *At Seventeen* for free, then decided they wanted more information. Of those 100 people (and these are only the ones who let us know how they'd found the site), 15 bought CDs. Not huge sales, right? No record company is interested in 180 extra sales a year. But . . . that translates into $2700, which is a lot of money in my book. And that doesn't include the ones who bought the CDs in stores, or who came to my shows.

> *The premise of all this ballyhoo is that the industry (and its artists) are being harmed by free downloading. Nonsense.*

Or take author Mercedes Lackey, who occupies entire shelves in stores and libraries. As she said herself: "For the past ten years, my three 'Arrows' books, which were published by DAW about 15 years ago, have been generating a nice, steady royalty check per pay-period each. A reasonable amount, for fifteen-year-old books. However . . . I just got the first half of my DAW royalties. . . . And suddenly, out of nowhere, each Arrows book has paid me three times the normal amount! . . . And because those books have never been out of print, and have always been promoted along with the rest of the backlist, the only significant change during that pay-period was something that happened over at Baen, one of my other publishers. That was when I had my co-author Eric Flint put the first of my Baen books on the Baen Free Library site. Because I have significantly more books with DAW than with Baen, the increases showed up at DAW first. There's an increase in all of the books on that statement, actually, and what it looks like is what I'd expect to happen if a steady line of people who'd never read my stuff encountered it on the Free Library—a certain percentage of them liked it, and started to work through my backlist, beginning with the earliest books published. The really interesting thing is, of course, that these aren't Baen books, they're DAW—another publisher—so it's 'name loyalty' rather than 'brand loyalty.' I'll tell you what, I'm sold. Free works."

In the hysteria of the moment, everyone is forgetting the main way an artist becomes successful— exposure.

I've found that to be true myself; every time we make a few songs available on my website, sales of all the CDs go up. A lot.

And I don't know about you, but as an artist with an in-print record catalogue that dates back to 1965, I'd be *thrilled* to see sales on my old catalogue rise.

The recording industry's problems

Now, RIAA and NARAS, as well as most of the entrenched music industry, are arguing that free downloads hurt sales. (More than hurt—they're saying it's destroying the industry.)

Alas, the music industry needs no outside help to destroy itself. We're doing a very adequate job of that on our own, thank you.

Here are a few statements from the RIAA's website:

1. "Analysts report that just one of the many peer-to-peer systems in operation is responsible for over 1.8 billion unauthorized downloads per month." (Hilary B. Rosen letter to the Honorable Rick Boucher, Congressman, February 28, 2002)
2. "Sales of blank CD-R discs have . . . grown nearly 2½ times in the last two years . . . if just half the blank discs sold in 2001 were used to copy music, the number of burned CDs worldwide is about the same as the number of CDs sold at retail." (Hilary B. Rosen letter to the Honorable Rick Boucher, Congressman, February 28, 2002)
3. "Music sales are already suffering from the impact . . . in the United States, sales decreased by more than 10% in 2001." (Hilary B. Rosen letter to the Honorable Rick Boucher, Congressman, February 28, 2002)
4 "In a recent survey of music consumers, 23% . . . said they are not

buying more music because they are downloading or copying their music for free." (Hilary B. Rosen letter to the Honorable Rick Boucher, Congressman, February 28, 2002)

Let's take these points one by one, but before that, let me remind you of something: the music industry had *exactly* the same response to the advent of reel-to-reel home tape recorders, cassettes, DATs, minidiscs, VHS, BETA, music videos ("Why buy the record when you can tape it?"), MTV, and a host of other technological advances designed to make the consumer's life easier and better. I know because I was there.

The only reason they didn't react that way publicly to the advent of CDs was because *they believed CD's were uncopyable.* I was told this personally by a former head of Sony marketing, when they asked me to license *Between the Lines* in CD format at a reduced royalty rate. ("Because it's a brand new technology.")

1. Who's to say that any of those people would have bought the CD's if the songs weren't available for free? I can't find a single study on this, one where a reputable surveyor such as Gallup actually asks people that question. I think no one's run one because everyone is afraid of the truth—most of the downloads are people who want to try an artist out, or who can't find the music in print.

   And if a percentage of that 1.8 billion is because people are downloading a current hit by Britney or In Sync, who's to say it really hurt their sales? Soft statistics are easily manipulated. How many of those people went out and bought an album that had been overplayed at radio for months, just because they downloaded a portion of it?

2. Sales of blank CDs have grown? You bet. I bought a new Vaio in December (ironically enough, made by Sony), and now back up all my files onto CD. I go through 7–15 CD's a week that way, or about 500 a year. Most new PC's come with XP, which makes backing up to CD painless; how many people are doing what I'm doing? Additionally, when I buy a new CD, I make a copy for my car, a copy for upstairs, and a copy for my partner. That's three blank discs per CD. So I alone account for around 750 blank CDs yearly.

3. I'm sure the sales decrease had nothing to do with the economy's decrease, or a steady downward spiral in the music industry, or the garbage being pushed by record companies. Aren't you? There were *32,000 new titles* released in this country in 2001, and that's not including re-issues, DIY's, or smaller labels that don't report to SoundScan. Our "Unreleased" series, which we haven't bothered SoundScanning, sold 6,000+ copies last year. A conservative estimate would place the number of "newly available" CD's per year at 100,000. That's an awful lot of releases for an industry that's being destroyed. And to make matters worse, we hear music everywhere, whether we want to or not; stores, amusement parks, highway rest stops. The original concept of Muzak (to be played in elevators so quietly that its soothing effect would be subliminal) has run amok. Why buy records when you can learn the entire Top 40 just by going shopping for groceries?

4. Which music consumers? College kids who can't afford to buy 10 new CDs a month, but want to hear their favorite groups? When I

bought my nephews a new Backstreet Boys CD, I asked why they hadn't downloaded it instead. They patiently explained to their senile aunt that the download wouldn't give them the cool artwork, and more important, the video they could see only on the CD.

Consumers want easier access to music

Realistically, why do most people download music? *To hear new music, or records that have been deleted and are no longer available for purchase.* Not to avoid paying $5 at the local used CD store, or taping it off the radio, but to hear music they can't find anywhere else. Face it—most people can't afford to spend $15.99 to experiment. Thats why listening booths (which labels fought against, too) are such a success.

You can't hear new music on radio these days; I live in Nashville, "Music City USA", and we have exactly one station willing to play a non-top-40 format. On a clear day, I can even tune it in. The situation's not much better in Los Angeles or New York. College stations are sometimes bolder, but their wattage is so low that most of us can't get them.

One other major point: in the hysteria of the moment, everyone is forgetting the main way an artist becomes successful—*exposure.* Without exposure, no one comes to shows, no one buys CDs, no one enables you to earn a living doing what you love. Again, from personal experience: in 37 years as a recording artist, I've created 25+ albums for major labels, and I've *never once* received a royalty check that didn't show I owed *them* money. So I make the bulk of my living from live touring, playing for 80–1500 people a night, doing my own show. I spend hours each week doing press, writing articles, making sure my website tour information is up to date. Why? Because all of that gives me exposure to an audience that might not come otherwise. So when someone writes and tells me they came to my show because they'd downloaded a song and gotten curious, I am thrilled!

It's dreadful to think that consumers are being asked to take responsibility for the industry's problems.

Who gets hurt by free downloads? Save a handful of super-successes like Celine Dion, none of us.

We only get helped.

But not to hear Congress tell it. Senator Fritz Hollings, chairman of the Senate Commerce Committee studying this, said "When Congress sits idly by in the face of these [file-sharing] activities, we essentially sanction the Internet as a haven for thievery", then went on to charge "over 10 million people" with stealing. That's what we think of consumers—they're thieves, out to get something for nothing.

Baloney. Most consumers have no problem paying for entertainment. One has only to look at the success of Fictionwise.com and the few other websites offering books and music at reasonable prices to understand that. If the music industry had a shred of sense, they'd have addressed this problem seven years ago, when people like Michael Camp were trying to obtain legitimate licenses for music online. Instead, the industry-wide attitude was *"It'll go away"*. That's the same attitude CBS Records had about rock 'n' roll when Mitch Miller was head of A&R. (And you wondered why they passed on The Beatles and The Rolling Stones.)

The recording industry's hypocrisy

I don't blame the RIAA for Hollings's attitude. They are, after all, the *Recording Industry* Association of America, formed so the labels would have a lobbying group in Washington. (In other words, they're permitted to make contributions to politicians and their parties.) But given that our industry's success is based on communication, the industry response to the Internet has been abysmal. Statements like the one above do nothing to help the cause.

Of course, communication has always been the artist's job, not the executives. That's why it's so scary when people like current NARAS president Michael Greene begin using shows like the Grammy Awards to drive their point home.

Grammy viewership hit a six-year low in 2002. Personally, I found the program so scintillating that it made me long for Rob Lowe dancing with Snow White, which at least was so bad that it was entertaining. Moves like the ridiculous Elton John–Eminem duet did little to make people want to watch again the next year. And we're not going to go into the *Los Angeles Times'* Pulitzer Prize–winning series on Greene and NARAS, where they pointed out that MusiCares has spent less than 10% of its revenue on disbursing emergency funds for people in the music industry (its primary purpose), or that Greene recorded his own album, pitched it to record executives while discussing Grammy business, then negotiated a $250,000 contract with Mercury Records for it (later withdrawn after the public flap). Or that NARAS quietly paid out at least $650,000 to settle a sexual harassment suit against him, a portion of which the non-profit Academy paid. Or that he's paid two million dollars a year, along with "perks" like his million-dollar country club membership and Mercedes. (Though it does make one wonder when he last entered a record store and bought something with his own hard-earned money.)

For those of us with major label contracts who want some of our music available for free downloading . . . well, the record companies . . . won't allow it.

Let's just note that in his speech he told the viewing audience that NARAS and RIAA were, in large part, taking their stance to protect artists. He hired three teenagers to spend a couple of days doing nothing but downloading, and they managed to download "6,000 songs". Come on. For free "front-row seats" at the Grammys and an appearance on national TV, I'd download twice that amount! But . . . who's got time to download that many songs? Does Greene really think people out there are spending twelve hours a day downloading our music? If they are, they must be starving to death, because they're not making a living or going to school.

How many of us can afford a T-1 line?

This sort of thing is indicative of the way statistics and information are being tossed around. It's dreadful to think that consumers are being asked to take responsibility for the industry's problems, which have been around far longer than the Internet. It's even worse to think that the consumer is being told they are charged with protecting us, the artists, when our own industry squanders the dollars we earn on waste and personal vendettas.

Greene went on to say that "Many of the nominees here tonight, especially the new, less-established artists, are in immediate danger of being marginalized out of our business." Right. Any "new" artist who manages to make the Grammys has millions of dollars in record company money behind them. The "real" new artists aren't people you're going to see on national TV, or hear on most radio. They're people you'll hear because someone gave you a disc, or they opened at a show you attended, or were lucky enough to be featured on NPR or another program still open to playing records that aren't already hits.

As to artists being "marginalized out of our business," the only people being marginalized out are the employees of our . . . record companies, who are being fired in droves because the higher-ups are incompetent.

The problems with CDs

And it's difficult to convince an educated audience that artists and record labels are about to go down the drain because they, the consumer, are downloading music. Particularly when they're paying $50–$125 apiece for concert tickets, and $15.99 for a new CD they know costs less than a couple of dollars to manufacture and distribute.

I suspect Greene thinks of downloaders as the equivalent of an old-style television drug dealer, lurking next to playgrounds, wearing big coats and whipping them open for wide-eyed children who then purchase black market CD's at generous prices.

What's the new industry byword? *Encryption.* They're going to make sure no one can copy CDs, even for themselves, or download them for free. Brilliant, except that it flouts previous court decisions about blank cassettes, blank videotapes, etc. And it pisses people off.

How many of you know that many car makers are now manufacturing all their CD players to also play DVD's? or that part of the encryption record companies are using doesn't allow your store-bought CD to be played on a DVD player, because that's the same technology as your computer? And if you've had trouble playing your own self-recorded copy of *O Brother Where Art Thou* in the car, it's because of this lunacy.

The industry's answer is to put on the label: "This audio CD is protected against unauthorized copying. It is designed to play in standard audio CD players and computers running Windows O/S; however, playback problems may be experienced. If you experience such problems, return this disc for a refund."

Now I ask you. After three or four experiences like that, *shlepping* to the store to buy it, then *shlepping* back to return it (and you still don't have your music), who's going to bother buying CD's?

The industry has been complaining for years about the stranglehold the middle-man has on their dollars, yet they wish to do nothing to offend those middle-men. (BMG has a strict policy for artists buying their own CDs to sell at concerts—$11 per CD. They know very well that most of us lose money if we have to pay that much; the point is to keep the big record stores happy by ensuring sales go to them. What actually happens is no sales to us *or* the stores.) NARAS and RIAA are moaning about the little mom & pop stores being shoved out of business; no one worked harder to shove them out than our own industry, which greeted every new Tower or mega-music store with glee, and offered steep discounts to Target and WalMart et al for stocking CDs. The Internet has zero to do with store closings and lowered sales.

And for those of us with major label contracts who *want* some of our music available for free downloading . . . well, the record companies own our masters, our outtakes, even our demos, and they won't allow it. Furthermore, they own our *voices* for the duration of the contract, so we can't even post a live track for downloading!

> *Free downloading gives a chance to every do-it-yourselfer out there.*

If you think about it, the music industry should be rejoicing at this new technological advance! Here's a fool-proof way to deliver music to millions who might otherwise never purchase a CD in a store. The cross-marketing opportunities are unbelievable. It's instantaneous, costs are minimal, shipping non-existent . . . a staggering vehicle for higher earnings and lower costs. Instead, they're running around like chickens with their heads cut off, bleeding on everyone and making no sense. As an alternative to encrypting everything, and tying up money for years (potentially decades) fighting consumer suits demanding their first amendment rights be protected (which have always gone to the consumer, as witness the availability of blank and unencrypted VHS tapes and casettes), why not take a tip from book publishers and writers?

Baen Free Library is one success story. SFWA [the Science Fiction and Fantasy Writers of America] is another. The SFWA site is one of the best out there for hands-on advice to writers, featuring in depth articles about everything from agent and publisher scams, to a continuously updated series of reports on various intellectual property issues. More important, many of the science fiction writers it represents have been heavily involved in the Internet since its inception. Each year, when the science fiction community votes for the Hugo and Nebula Awards (their equivalent of the Grammys), most of the works nominated are put on the site in their entirety, allowing voters *and* non-voters the opportunity to peruse them. Free. If you are a member or associate (at a nominal fee), you have access to even more works. The site is also full of links to members' own web pages and on-line stories, even when they aren't nominated for anything. Reading this material, again for free, allows browsers to figure out which writers they want to find more of—and buy their books. Wouldn't it be nice if all the records nominated for awards each year were available for free downloading, even if it were only the winners? People who hadn't bought the albums might actually listen to the singles, then go out and purchase the records.

The real issues facing artists

I have no objection to Greene et al trying to protect the record labels, who are the ones fomenting this hysteria. RIAA is funded by them. NARAS is supported by them. *However, I object violently to the pretense that they are in any way doing this for our benefit.* If they really wanted to do something for the great majority of artists, who eke out a living against all odds, they could tackle some of the real issues facing us:

- The normal industry contract is for seven albums, with no end date, which would be considered at best indentured servitude (and at worst slavery) in any other business. In fact, it would be illegal.
- A label can shelve your project, then extend your contract by one more album because what you turned in was "commercially or artistically unacceptable". They alone determine that criteria.
- Singer-songwriters have to accept the "Controlled Composition Clause" (which dictates that they'll be paid only 75% of the rates set by Congress in publishing royalties) for any major or subsidiary label recording contract, or lose the contract. Simply put, the clause demanded by the labels provides that a) if you write your own songs, you will only be paid 3/4 of what Congress has told the record companies they must pay you, and b) if you co-write, you will use your "best efforts" to ensure that other songwriters accept the 75% rate as well. If they refuse, you must agree to make up the difference out of your share.
- Congressionally set writer/publisher royalties have risen from their 1960's high (2 cents per side) to a munificent 8 cents.
- Many of us began in the 50's and 60's; our records are still in release, and we're still being paid royalty rates of 2% (if anything) on them.
- If we're not songwriters, and not hugely successful commercially (as in platinum-plus), we don't make a dime off our recordings. Recording industry accounting procedures are right up there with films.
- Worse yet, when records go out-of-print, we don't get them back! We can't even take them to another company. Careers have been deliberately killed in this manner, with the record company refusing to release product or allow the artist to take it somewhere else.
- And because a record label "owns" your voice for the duration of the contract, you can't go somewhere else and re-record those same songs they turned down.
- And because of the re-record provision, even after your contract is over, you can't record those songs for someone else for years, and sometimes decades.
- Last but not least, America is the only country I am aware of that pays no live performance royalties to songwriters. In Europe, Japan, Australia, when you finish a show, you turn your set list in to the promoter, who files it with the appropriate organization, and then pays a small royalty per song to the writer. It costs the singer nothing, the rates are based on venue size, and it ensures that writers

whose songs no longer get airplay, but are still performed widely, can continue receiving the benefit from those songs.

Additionally, we should be speaking up, and Congress should be listening. At this point they're only hearing from multi-platinum acts. What about someone like Ani Difranco, one of the most trusted voices in college entertainment today? What about those of us who live most of our lives outside the big corporate system, and who might have very different views on the subject?

There is *zero* evidence that material available for free online downloading is financially harming anyone. In fact, most of the hard evidence is to the contrary.

Greene and the RIAA are correct in one thing—these are times of great change in our industry. But at a time when there are arguably only four record labels left in America (Sony, AOL/Time/Warner, Universal, BMG—and where is the RICO [Racketeering Influenced and Corrupt Organizations] act when we need it?) . . . when entire *genres* are glorifying the gangster mentality and losing their biggest voices to violence . . . when executives change positions as often as Zsa Zsa Gabor changed clothes, and "A&R" has become a euphemism for "Absent & Redundant" . . . well, we have other things to worry about.

It's absurd for us, as artists, to sanction—or countenance—the shutting down of something like this. It's sheer stupidity to rejoice at the Napster decision. Short-sighted, and ignorant.

Free exposure is practically a thing of the past for entertainers. Getting your record played at radio costs more money than most of us dream of ever earning. Free downloading gives a chance to every do-it-yourselfer out there. Every act that can't get signed to a major, for whatever reason, can reach literally millions of new listeners, enticing them to buy the CD and come to the concerts. Where else can a new act, or one that doesn't have a label deal, get that kind of exposure?

Please note that I am *not* advocating indiscriminate downloading without the artist's permission. I am *not* saying copyrights are meaningless. I am objecting to the RIAA spin that they are doing this to protect "the artists", and make us more money. I am annoyed that so many records I once owned are out of print, and the only place I could find them was Napster. Most of all, I'd like to see an end to the hysteria that causes a group like RIAA to spend over 45 million dollars in 2001 lobbying "on our behalf", when every record company out there is complaining that they have no money.

We'll turn into Microsoft if we're not careful, folks, insisting that any household wanting an extra copy for the car, the kids, or the portable CD player, has to go out and "license" multiple copies.

As artists, we have the ear of the masses. We have the trust of the masses. By speaking out in our concerts and in the press, we can do a great deal to damp this hysteria, and put the blame for the sad state of our industry right back where it belongs—in the laps of record companies, radio programmers, and our own apparent inability to organize ourselves in order to better our own lives—and those of our fans. If we don't take the reins, no one will.

6

Online File Sharing Threatens the Film Industry

Jack Valenti

Jack Valenti is president of the Motion Picture Association of America, a trade organization that represents the American motion picture, home video, and television industries.

The movie industry, a large and important contributor to the American economy, is under attack from online pirates who illegally download thousands of movies every day. The movie industry is making efforts to educate the public about the harms of movie piracy, but at the same time new technologies are making it increasingly easy for online movie piracy to flourish. In addition to the economic harms associated with online piracy, there are social harms, since peer-to-peer file-sharing networks are often used to spread pornography.

No nation can lay claim to greatness or longevity unless it constructs a rostrum from which springs a "moral imperative" which guides the daily conduct of its citizens. Within the core of that code of conduct is a simple declaration that to take something that does not belong to you not only is wrong, but it is a clear violation of the moral imperative, which is fastened deep in all religions.

That is fundamental to how this nation fits itself to honorable conduct. Anyone who deals in infirm logic to certify that "stealing movies off the Internet is okay, nothing wrong about it since everybody does it, and no one gets hurt," is obviously offering up a defunct mythology to cover their tracks.

Piracy, or "stealing," is the darker side of digital subversion. Digital theft has an inevitable leaning toward a future darkly seen by those who create, distribute and market films. For the almost one million men and women who work in some aspect of the movie industry—99 percent of whom don't make big salaries, who are good citizens and good neighbors, with mortgages to pay and kids to send to college—their livelihood is per-

Jack Valenti, testimony before the Senate Committee on Commerce, Science, and Transportation, Washington, DC, September 17, 2003.

ilously in doubt if digital stealing goes on, increasing in velocity with a casual disregard for other people's intellectual property.

Intellectual property nourishes the American economy

Piracy is a national problem. It must be a high priority of the officials who comprise the federal government. Intellectual property (movies, TV programs, home video, books, music, and computer software) is an awesome engine of growth which nourishes the national economy. Not only is intellectual property America's largest trade export, bringing in more international revenues than agriculture, aircraft, automobiles and auto parts, but it is creating new jobs at three times the rate of the rest of the economy and is responsible for over five percent of the GDP [gross domestic product]. The movie industry alone has a surplus balance of trade with every single country in the world. No other American enterprise can make that statement—and at a time when this country is bleeding from a $400 billion–plus deficit balance of trade.

Filching movies in digital form by uploading and downloading on the Net, is not only just plain wrong, but has a malignant effect on the future of American consumers.

The movie industry sits on a fragile fiscal bottom. Only one in ten films ever gets its investment returned through theatrical exhibition. Films have to journey through many market venues—premium and basic cable, satellite delivery, home video, network and individual TV stations, international—in order to try to recoup the private risk capital that brings a movie to life. If a film is kidnapped early in that journey, it's obvious the worth of that film can be fatally depleted long before it can retrieve its investment.

At this moment, the movie industry is suffering from a loss of some $3.5 billion annually from hard-goods piracy—DVD, VCD, videotape. We are every hour of every day fighting that theft all over the world. As yet, we have not put a loss-figure on digital piracy. We are working on it. We do know from outside estimates that some 400,000 to 600,000 films are being stolen every day, and it is getting progressively worse.

Educating the public

The movie industry is laboring to find rebuttals to piracy. We have launched an education project through TV public service announcements, trailers in theaters, an alliance with one million students via Junior Achievement to 'explain and educate' why copyright is central to intellectual property growth, and why filching movies in digital form by uploading and downloading on the Net, is not only just plain wrong, but has a malignant effect on the future of American consumers.

We are also launching a long-term technological research project enlisting the finest brains in the high tech industry to discover ways and means to baffle piracy, technologically. We are constantly looking for innovative and robust ways to protect American creative works which, I am proud to report, finds a hospitable reception on all the continents where our films are patronized and enjoyed by all creeds, cultures and countries.

That is why I am here today—to tell you of the immeasurable economic and entertainment value of American films—and to ask for your help in the never-ceasing fight to combat theft of our movies.

No one can predict the future

I don't know, nor does anyone else, the shape and form of the future. We do know that the technology we find so magical today will seem primitive 12 to 18 months from now. The ascending curve of change is mindbending. But no one can chart the digital future.

That is why to impose an absolute congressional exile on so-called "technology mandates" is not good public policy. No one can forecast what future technology mandates will be needed. That's why it is not in the national interest to ban what you cannot see, to prohibit what you do not know, to turn your back on what you cannot measure.

An absolute ban on technology mandates for access control or redistribution control technologies would injure the discretion of the FCC [Federal Communications Commission]. It is an agency created by Congress to regulate in the public interest. To do that it needs the tools to do the job, to carry out its legislative command. Expert agencies like the FCC were created to take on the burden of detailed, abstruse regulations that Congress has agreed it is not equipped to do. To tie the FCC's hand in advance is surely not in the public interest.

Is the Congress familiar with experiments now going on that will reshape and enlarge the ease and speed of digital thievery?

I agree that the proposed ban on technology mandates cheers those whose mantra is "all content must be free," including pornography and material stolen from its owners. But their view collides with the public interest.

The FCC should have the authority to adopt regulations that serve the interests of consumers. That may very well include technical mandates that would create a safe environment in which valuable content would be made available in vast amounts to consumers. . . .

Our most anxious concerns are not about the present, but the future. Is the Congress familiar with experiments now going on that will reshape and enlarge the ease and speed of digital thievery? Cal Tech reported one experiment called "FAST," which can download a quality DVD movie in five seconds! Another experiment, "Internet-2," has dispatched 6.7 gigabytes halfway around the world in one minute! (A DVD-movie contains some 4.6 gigabytes.) What is experiment today will be commonplace in the community three to four years from now. Which means that the glorious enticement of *free* and easy uploading and downloading movies, with little risk will be far more intense than it is now.

Pornographic content on the Internet

This Committee must be sensitive to a most unwholesome fungus which infests "peer-to-peer file swapping sites" such as Gnutella, Morpheus, KaZaa, iMesh, E Donkey, Grockster, etc. That disfiguring fungus is pornography on a scale so squalid it will shake the very core of your being. As easy as it is to illegally download movies, it is equally easy to bring home this foul pornography. Any 10-year-old can do it—and probably does. Do parents know this?

While searching for pirated material on these P2P sites, MPAA [Motion Picture Association of America] technicians discovered large caches of pornography disguised as child-friendly fare. This awful content is "meta-tagged" or coded to searches children are likely to undertake, like "Disney," "Harry Potter," or "Spy Kids." Is it the intent of this Committee to ban expert agencies from mandating technical remedies yet to be found to allow parents to fence off this foul material from their children?

What the movie industry needs

We need the Congress to understand and appreciate the vast worth of copyrighted intellectual property. In the global film arena the United States is preeminent. We need the Congress to heed our warnings that unless there is put in place various baffle-plates of protection, we will bear witness to the slow undoing of this huge economic and creative force.

Which is why I urge the Congress not to close the legislative door on any new technological magic that has the capacity to combat digital thievery which—if unchecked—will drown the movie industry in ever-increasing levels of piracy.

7

The Government Should Explore Ways of Making File Sharing Legal

Electronic Frontier Foundation

The Electronic Frontier Foundation (EFF) is an advocacy organization that works to defend civil liberties and individual rights, primarily in cases where legal and technological issues intersect.

The controversy over online music sharing shows that the United States' current system of copyrights laws—which makes it illegal to share music files via peer-to-peer (P2P) networks—is easily circumvented by modern technology. Rather than trying to force everyone, through lawsuits and other means, to conform to an outdated copyright system, the United States should implement a licensing scheme under which artists can be compensated for the dissemination of their work online. In much the same way that artists agree to let radio stations play their songs for a prearranged, fixed fee, so too could artists voluntarily license their works to P2P networks. Unfortunately, record companies have resisted voluntary licensing schemes. An alternative is compulsory licensing: Congress could force the music industry to adopt a system under which online music sharing is legal, but the administrators of P2P networks or Internet service providers are required to share profits with copyright holders.

It's time to face the fact that in today's world, copyright law is broken. Our current copyright regime makes criminals out of music lovers. Worse, it makes suspected criminals out of all Internet users.

Congress has given copyright holders expanded subpoena powers similar to those granted to government officials under the USA PATRIOT Act [passed to aid the war on terrorism in fall 2001]. This means that whether or not you use peer-to-peer [P2P] file-sharing programs, the recording industry (or anyone who claims to be a rights-holder!) can easily gain access to your personal information—without a judge's oversight.

Industry representatives say that the subpoenas and lawsuits are necessary to protect recording artists. But suing fans doesn't pay artists. Neither does threatening every Internet user's civil liberties. We need a constructive solution. EFF [Electronic Frontier Foundation] advocates offering fans a legal way to use P2P programs while ensuring that artists get paid.

EFF advocates offering fans a legal way to use P2P programs while ensuring that artists get paid.

P2P holds significant potential for both artists and fans, but it can't fully be realized until the lawsuits stop. We've seen this story many times with new technology and old media, so the solution is no mystery: we need a licensing plan for P2P. Think of a license as a shield from lawsuits. Here are a couple of ways to get legal:

Voluntary Collective Licensing

Copyright holders could voluntarily join together and offer "blanket" licenses, also known as "Voluntary Collective Licensing."

This is how the "problem" of radio was ultimately resolved (only after copyright owners gave up on trying to sue it out of existence, of course). A "performing rights organization" (PRO) was formed, songwriters and music publishers were invited to join, and blanket licenses were given to any and all radio stations that wanted them.

Today, there are three major PROs in the United States—ASCAP [American Society of Composers, Authors, and Publishers], BMI [Broadcast Music, Inc.], and SESAC [a PRO]. In exchange for a fee, they will give blanket licenses to anyone who asks. (For antitrust reasons, the terms offered by ASCAP and BMI are closely monitored by a federal court.) Once licensed, radio stations may play anything, anytime, without having to ask permission first. The PROs then divide up the fees among their members.

This solution does not require any changes to copyright law and leaves price-setting to the copyright owners. Something much like this could be developed for file-sharing. Copyright owners could get together and offer blanket licenses on nondiscriminatory terms, either to ISPs, software vendors, or consumers directly.

The problem, of course, is that this solution has been available to copyright owners all along. It only works if virtually all copyright owners join and forgo lawsuits in exchange for a reasonable piece of the pie. So far, the big entertainment companies have shown no interest in pursuing a voluntary "collective licensing" plan.

Compulsory licensing

What happens if copyright holders refuse to grant licenses at any price? It wouldn't be the first time; this situation arose with player pianos, cable TV, satellite TV, digital recording media, and Internet radio as well. Traditionally, however, the government has stepped into the fray and "compelled" copyright holders to license their work for a fee. This is called a "compulsory license" (or "compulsory").

The first American compulsory was adopted when the music industry fought the Napster of 1909: the player piano. Sheet music publishers claimed that the creation of piano-readable sheets was against the law and that they should have the right to monopolize the booming piano roll industry. Congress disagreed and instead crafted a compulsory license that paid recording artists while protecting the new technology. Today, this license allows bands to record (or "cover") another band's song (so long as they've paid the $.08 per copy of the recorded track).

While a compulsory always requires copyright holders to make their works available for fair compensation, the particular method of compensation is totally open. In the world of Internet radio, for instance, a webcaster pays for the songs that she plays. Her fees and playlists go to a central distribution point, and the artists on the playlists are compensated. On the other hand, cable TV companies pay broadcast networks directly when they play network programming like "The Simpsons."

This kind of licensing has often been necessary. When copyright holders can't reach consensus on licensing terms, Congress has properly stepped in to move things forward.

8

The Government Must Combat Online Piracy

Bonnie J.K. Richardson

Bonnie J.K. Richardson is the vice president of trade and federal affairs for the Motion Picture Association of America.

Intellectual property such as movies and music is easily stolen over the Internet. The U.S. government must work to ensure that intellectual property rights are not threatened by copyright theft over the Internet. International laws have helped to protect intellectual property rights, but many of these are harmful to America because the laws run counter to U.S. regulations. Therefore, it is necessary that the U.S. government step in to protect the rights of artists.

I am testifying on behalf of the Motion Picture Association of America. MPAA is a trade association representing seven of the major producers and distributors of filmed and digital entertainment for exhibition in theaters, for home entertainment and for television. Our members include Buena Vista Pictures Distribution, Inc. (A Walt Disney Company), Metro-Goldwyn-Mayer Studios Inc., Paramount Pictures Corporation, Sony Pictures Entertainment Inc., Twentieth Century Fox Film Corporation, Universal City Studios, Inc., and Warner Bros., a division of AOL Time Warner.

Copyright revenue

As many of you may already know, the content industries— movies, television programming, home video, music publishing, computer games and software—are America's most successful exporters. These copyright-based industries generate more revenues internationally than any other US industry— more than aircraft, more than agriculture, more than automobiles and auto parts. We also create jobs in the United States at three times the rate of the rest of the economy. As Jack Valenti, President and CEO of the Motion Picture Association of America, is fond of saying, the copyright industries are "the jewel in America's trade crown."

Digital networks offer new opportunities for delivering our entertain-

Bonnie J.K. Richardson, testimony before the House Subcommittee on Commerce, Trade, and Consumer Protection, Committee on Commerce, Washington, DC, May 22, 2001.

ment products in international markets. In [2001,] several movie studios will launch new, encrypted on-line services. No one knows today which business model, or models, will prove most successful in getting digitized entertainment content to customers, but we may start to get some answers in the next few months.

The one thing I can tell you is that all of those business models for the digital delivery of content—at home and abroad—depend on successfully protecting the content against theft.

Internet piracy

Internet piracy is the single biggest impediment to digital trade today. Piracy of copyrighted materials is not a new problem. In the last quarter century, MPAA and its associated anti-piracy organizations have spent a billion dollars fighting video piracy and signal theft around the world. At present, we have anti-piracy programs in over 80 countries. What is new in the fight against piracy in the Internet era is the speed and ease with which our products can be stolen and distributed illegally over digital networks. Today, Viant (a Boston-based consulting firm) estimates that some 350,000 movies are being downloaded illegally every day. By the end of [2001], they estimate that as many as one million illegal movie downloads will take place every single day. The scale of the problem is unprecedented.

Internet piracy is the single biggest impediment to digital trade today.

We have some new tools for combating copyright theft. At the end of 1996 the World Intellectual Property Organization (WIPO) adopted two new treaties to bring copyright standards into the digital age. These treaties clarify exclusive rights in the on-line world and prohibit circumvention of technological protection measures for copyrighted works. The United States Congress implemented those treaties over two years ago in the Digital Millennium Copyright Act. Unfortunately, other countries have not acted quite as swiftly, and the treaties are still not in effect. Twenty-four countries have deposited their instruments of ratification of the WIPO Copyright Treaty; 22 countries have completed the ratification process for the WIPO Performances and Phonograms Treaty. We hope to reach the 30-country mark before the end of the summer so the treaties can enter into effect. [The treaty took effect on March 6, 2002.] Of course, even after the treaties enter into force, we will continue working to get all countries to adhere to these important principles. One of the disturbing truths in the e-commerce world is that piracy flows to the country where the levels of protection are the lowest; even the tiniest country can be the source of extraordinary levels of damage.

Meanwhile, we support the efforts of the Administration to ensure that the standards set in the WIPO treaties and the standards in the Digital Millennium Copyright Act are incorporated into free trade agreements, including those with Singapore, Chile, and the Free Trade Agreement of the Americas.

Swift and vigorous enforcement of copyright laws by countries around the globe is also essential. Tools provided by Congress for ensuring effective enforcement of intellectual property laws remain extremely important for ensuring that countries abroad provide effective enforcement against piracy. These tools include Special 301 and other trade-related legislation, including the Generalized System of Preference (GSP), the Caribbean Basic Economic Recovery Act, the Caribbean Basin Trade Partnership Act, the Andean Trade Preferences Act, and the African Growth Opportunities Act.

Questions of jurisdiction

The Hague Convention is also attempting to tackle issues that are very important to any company that engages in international commerce. When laws are broken, which country or countries have jurisdiction over the infractions and where can the judgments be enforced? The Hague Convention is attempting to complete an international instrument to address these questions in a global fashion.[1]

The questions of jurisdiction are especially complex in the e-commerce world. What factors should determine where a transaction or resulting injuries took place? Is it where the company is headquartered? Where the server is located? Where the customer is located? Does it matter whether or not the service is being advertised or directly marketed to customers in a particular country? Does the language in which the service is being offered indicate intent, or lack thereof, to conduct business in a particular country? What does it mean to "target" activities toward a particular forum, and how do U.S. notions of minimum contacts and purposeful availment work in the online environment?

With your continued vigilance and support . . .
America's "crown jewels" continue to sparkle
brightly in the digital age.

Because copyright theft is such a pervasive international problem—particularly in the Internet environment—and because we rely on courts around the world to help bring pirates to justice, the copyright industries have been particularly concerned about the new rules being formulated by the Hague Convention. A common-sense convention on jurisdiction and the enforcement of foreign judgments could have some benefit to the copyright industries in confronting global infringements, and we support the United States' efforts to reach such a common-sense solution. Unfortunately, the operative draft of the Convention is painted with a broad brush that reflects the fact that much of the discussion leading up to its creation occurred before the advent of e-commerce. As a result, and by failing to squarely address the types of difficult questions I just raised, the Draft Convention in its current form threatens to do more harm than good.

Some who oppose the treaty have focused on copyright as an exam-

---

1. As of August 2004, the Convention—in which dozens of nations, including the United States, are participating—had not yet finalized a treaty.

ple of why the Draft Convention is problematic. They point to differences in national law and the possibility that a judgment rendered in a foreign country based on foreign law will be enforced in the United States. They suggest that the solution is simply to excise intellectual property issues from this agreement. We do not view this as a good solution. The fact is that today—even in the absence of a global convention on jurisdiction—U.S. companies who engage in e-commerce must deal with differences in national laws and can be called into court in a foreign country to answer for acts that reach foreign countries. (The Yahoo! case on the sale of Nazi memorabilia in France is just one example).[2] On top of that, the U.S. is quite liberal in its recognition and enforcement of foreign judgments. This is happening today.

It is important to keep in mind that the Hague Convention doesn't try to resolve questions of substantive law. If substantive laws were the main question, copyright issues would be easier to address internationally than many other e-commerce related problems, such as illegal content or privacy. There is a greater degree of harmonization of copyright laws as a result of the Berne Convention and the WTO Trade-Related Aspects of Intellectual Property Rights (TRIPS) agreement[3] than is the case in many other areas of law and policy. The problem is jurisdiction: Will the Convention result in U.S. companies finding themselves subject to jurisdiction in a forum where they would not be subject to jurisdiction today, and would the Convention result in the enforcement of judgments that today would not be enforced?

These issues of jurisdiction underlie all kinds of tort actions and are of as much concern to other e-businesses as to the copyright industries. The problems cannot be resolved simply by excising intellectual property. The same questions remain with respect to cases for defamation, for hate speech, for privacy violations, for unfair trade practices, and for all other areas of non-harmonized law. We agree with others that the current Draft Convention inadequately addresses these questions, and we believe these questions must be answered with respect to all areas of the law if the Convention is to go forward. . . .

Government intervention is needed

I want to thank the members of this committee for your keen interest in the barriers that affect digital commerce. The American film, home entertainment and TV programming industry is the only industry in America today that enjoys a positive balance of trade with every country around the globe. Together with our colleagues in the music, books and software industries, we are America's leading exporter. With your continued vigilance and support, as you work with the Administration and with foreign governments, you can ensure that America's "crown jewels" continue to sparkle brightly in the digital age.

---

2. In May 2000, a French court ruled that Yahoo! must prevent residents of France from accessing sites that sell Nazi memorabilia.   3. The Berne Convention protects literary and artistic works, while the TRIPS agreement requires members of the World Trade Organization to enforce intellectual property rights.

9

The Music Industry's Lawsuits Against Online Music Sharers Are Justified

Mitch Bainwol

Mitch Bainwol is chairman and chief executive officer of the Recording Industry Association of America (RIAA), a trade organization that represents the music industry. In September 2003 the RIAA began filing lawsuits against hundreds of individuals who make files of copyrighted music available for download on the Internet.

The music industry has begun filing lawsuits against individuals who share music online after several years of declining music sales caused in part by rampant Internet piracy. Individuals who make copyrighted music accessible to millions of people through peer-to-peer networks are in clear violation of federal copyright laws. Nevertheless, P2P networks such as Kazaa encourage this form of piracy, and Internet service providers such as Verizon have been reluctant to work with the music industry to reduce online music sharing. The music industry has filed its lawsuits in accordance with the Digital Millennium Copyright Act (DMCA), and in obtaining information about individual file sharers, the industry has been careful to act in accordance with DMCA privacy safeguards.

My name is Mitch Bainwol. I am the Chairman and CEO of the Recording Industry Association of America, the trade association representing the U.S. recording industry. RIAA members create, manufacture and/or distribute 90 percent of all legitimate sound recordings in the United States.

I'd like to take this opportunity to provide . . . some background, insight and perspective on our multi-pronged efforts to combat the devastating effects that the massive illegal copying on peer-to-peer networks is having on the music industry. The problems currently facing the music industry will, as broadband expands, soon be the problems of all copyright holders. This is a point of national importance, as the copyright in-

Mitch Bainwol, testimony before the Senate Committee on Governmental Affairs, Washington, DC, September 30, 2003.

dustries constitute five percent of the Gross Domestic Product and copyrighted works are the single largest United States export.

The decision to enforce our rights against egregious infringers was taken only after suffering years of mounting harm and trying all other avenues. The music industry first tried to use an aggressive public education campaign to discourage the unauthorized distribution of recordings, by explaining to the public that online piracy is not only illegal, but robs songwriters and recording artists of their livelihoods, stifles the careers of up-and-coming musicians, and threatens the jobs of tens of thousands of less celebrated people in the music industry.

The decision [to file lawsuits] was taken only after suffering years of mounting harm and trying all other avenues.

The music industry also pursued lawsuits against the peer-to-peer systems, which are knowingly facilitating the illegal distribution of copyrighted recordings on a massive scale. Most important, the music industry has aggressively licensed legitimate online music services to offer legal alternatives to consumers. Only after these steps did not stem the tidal wave of illegal conduct has RIAA resorted to its current course, pursuing the users of peer-to-peer networks who are distributing substantial amounts of unauthorized copies of recordings. And there is one point on which all of the courts have agreed: these users are violating the copyright laws. Our heightened enforcement efforts are deliberately occurring now when, as a result of the music industry's extensive educational efforts, the public is more aware than ever before of the illegality and consequences of online piracy and, at the same time, the number of legitimate online music sources is exploding, giving music lovers a multitude of options for legally obtaining music online.

The piracy problem facing the music industry

In the past three years, shipments of recorded music in the United States have fallen by an astounding 26 percent, from 1.16 billion units in 1999 to 860 million units in 2002. And worldwide, the recording industry has shrunk from a $40 billion industry in 2000 down to a $32 billion industry in 2002. Hit records—which are critical to the long-term health of the music industry and enable investment in new artists and new music— have suffered most dramatically. In 2000, the ten top-selling albums in the United States sold a total of 60 million units. In 2001, that number dropped to 40 million. Last year, it totaled just 34 million.

The root cause for this drastic decline in record sales is the astronomical rate of music piracy on the Internet. Computer users illegally download more than 2.6 billion copyrighted files (mostly recordings) every month. At any given moment, well over five million users are online offering well over 1 billion files for copying through various peer-to-peer networks. Peer-to-peer networks allow a user to make media files, including recordings, stored on that user's computer available for copying by others; to search for media files stored on other users' computers; and to transfer exact copies of the contents of other users' media files to that user's own computer. A song can be copied and distributed in this manner an unlimited number of times, without any degradation in sound quality. And unlike traditional music piracy, piracy through networks is viral: unless the user takes affirmative steps to prevent it, the user automatically and immediately begins offering the files that the user copied to millions of other users. Moreover, the overwhelming majority of the distribution that occurs on peer-to-peer networks is unauthorized.

It is widely recognized and acknowledged that individuals who engage in such unauthorized distribution—either by making recordings available for others to copy or by making copies of others' files—are committing a clear violation of the copyright laws. The courts have been unanimous on this point. As the Ninth Circuit explained in the *Napster* case, "a majority of Napster users use the service to download and upload copyrighted music. . . . And by doing that, . . . the uses constitute direct infringement of plaintiffs' musical compositions, recordings." Judge [Stephen] Wilson quoted this language in the recent *Grokster* case, and similarly recognized that many Grokster and Streamcast users were downloading copyrighted music, "thereby infring[ing] [copyright owners'] rights of reproduction and distribution." Most recently, in a case involving Aimster. Judge [Richard A.] Posner of the Seventh Circuit noted that Aimster users who were distributing or making copies of copyrighted music were copyright infringers, and that there was no evidence in the record before him that Aimster "has ever been used for a noninfringing use."

> *The root cause for [the] drastic decline in record sales is the astronomical rate of music piracy on the Internet.*

According to a November 2002 survey by Peter D. Hart Research, by a nearly 2-to-1 margin, consumers who say they are illegally downloading more music report that they are purchasing less music. The same survey found that the main reason consumers are not buying more music is that they get a lot of what they want for free by illegally downloading or copying it from others. In a similar study conducted in May 2002 by Peter D. Hart Research, among 12- to 18-year-olds, 35 percent say the first thing they will do after hearing a new song that they like is download it, versus just 10 percent who will buy it. Among 19- to 24-year-olds, 32 percent download the new song first, versus 9 percent who will buy it.

These findings are bolstered by a June 2003 Edison Media Research report which found that "among the heaviest downloaders, 48% say they no longer have to buy CDs because they could download music for free over the Internet"—an increase of 61 percent in just one year. It is thus not surprising that, while sales of music CDs are dropping, sales of blank CDs (onto which downloaded recordings can be copied) have increased dramatically, by more than 30 percent in 2002. Sales of blank CDs now outstrip sales of music CDs by a more than 2-to-1 margin.

These findings are consistent with the skyrocketing number of users of peer-to-peer networks. As of July 2002, Kazaa—the most popular peer-to-peer network by far—boasted 100 million registered users. By May 2003, Kazaa had become the world's most downloaded software program of any kind, with 278 million downloads.

P2P networks encourage online piracy

Although these peer-to-peer networks are well aware of the rampant illegal copying that occurs over their systems, they have taken no concrete steps to stop it, and in fact, they encourage and enable that conduct, while at the same time taking steps to shield themselves from liability. They provide no meaningful warning to their users that uploading or downloading copyrighted recordings violates the law. They provide no filter to prevent exchange of copyrighted material, even though many provide filters that at least attempt to block pornography and viruses. Peer-to-peer networks also establish "default" settings that, unless affirmatively changed by the user, automatically make the files on the user's hard drive available for copying by anyone else on the network. And, as John Malcolm the Deputy Assistant Attorney General of the Criminal Division noted in testimony before the Judiciary Committee . . . , in order to foster anonymity on the network:

> many peer-to-peer networks do not require individual users to set up accounts with a central authority. Peer-to-peer users can change their names at will and the names that they choose rarely contain true information that would identify them.

As Judge Wilson observed in the movie and music industries' case against Grokster, Streamcast, and Kazaa, these peer-to-peer networks "may have intentionally structured their businesses to avoid secondary liability for copyright infringement, while benefiting financially from the illicit draw of their wares." Indeed, Kazaa has established itself in the country of Vanuatu, while the illegal activities on its network are causing the loss of numerous jobs in the music industry in the United States. Taken together, all of these factors are clear evidence that the Kazaa's of the world have done and will do anything within their power to facilitate copyright infringement and avoid accountability or legal liability for their actions.

Internet service providers benefit from piracy

Although Internet service providers, like Verizon and SBC, are in a unique position to educate their customers about the myriad of threats—legal, privacy, security—posed by using P2P systems, they have chosen instead to do nothing to educate or warn subscribers. For example, nowhere in Verizon's or SBC's brochures, websites, or advertising are there any warnings or information about the real legal risks associated with using P2P software to get free music. To the contrary, both SBC and Verizon have used a combination of overt and subtle marketing strategies to encourage people to sign up for DSL so they can get all the music they want for free and not have to go to the record store anymore.

The motivation for this strategy is clear when you look at the broadband landscape.

According to a recent *USA Today* article, 70% of Americans with broadband capabilities use cable modems instead of DSL. The same article quotes an Internet analyst saying: "It's going to be more streaming video and music downloading that's really going to dictate the switch—far more than the price." And a recent report on broadband found that the "growth in peer-to-peer is really driving the market, . . . [and] P2P traffic now consumes 50% to 70% of the capacity . . . up from perhaps 20% to 30% a year ago, . . .".

With a long way to go before catching up to cable, it's no wonder Verizon and SBC—the nation's two largest DSL providers—are reluctant participants in the fight against online piracy. Fortunately, for the copyright community, the vast majority of other ISPs around the nation have been responsible and constructive partners in this important fight.

It's difficult to discount the commercial interests of Verizon and SBC when weighing the merits of their arguments. After all, rather than focusing on the most pressing problems facing their customers, they champion protecting the anonymity of subscribers who are engaged in clearly illegal activity. So while millions of their users are breaking the law while exposing their most sensitive personal information to the world, Verizon and SBC want Congress to believe that the true threat to their consumers is the DMCA [Digital Millennium Copyright Act] information subpoena process and the RIAA, not the Kazaa's of the world. If Verizon and SBC spent as much time and resources educating their customers about the illegality of using P2P services to get free music as they have fighting the RIAA in Court and in Congress, the Internet piracy landscape might look a whole lot better.

The availability of legal online music

The widespread availability of free illegal copies to download through these peer-to-peer networks has greatly interfered with the development of legitimate online sources of music. But music lovers need not break the law to obtain their favorite music online. The music industry continues to respond to consumer demand by making its music available to a wide range of authorized online subscription, streaming, and download services that make it easier than ever for fans to get music legally on the Internet. There are now many legal and inexpensive ways to get music online. In the United States market alone, there are dozens of excellent legitimate online services that offer a variety of choices to enjoy and purchase online music. These services include: aolmusic.com, apple.com/music, audiocandy.com, bestbuy.com, bet.com, buymusic.com, catsmusic.com, CircuitCity.com, collegeconcerts.com, cornercd.com, dimple.com, dothehole.com, earwax.com, efetus.com, emusic.com, exitosmusical.com, facethemusic.com, fullaudio.com, FYE.com, galleryofsound.com, independentrecord.com, instavid.com, latinoise.com, liquid.com, burnitfirst.com, listen.com, mainstreetmusic.com, millenniummusic.com, miramag.com, mp3.com, mtv.com, musicmatch.com, musicmillennium.com, musicnet.com, musicrebellion.com, netscape.com/music, newworldrecord.com, phillysoulclassics.com, pressplay.com, qhut.com, rasputinmusic.com, real.com/realone/rhapsody, recordandtapetraders.com, rollingstone.com, samgoody.com, spinner.com, streamwaves.com, tophitsmusic.com, tow-errecords.com, windowsmedia.com.

Indeed, the number of legitimate online sources of music is continuing to increase. Additional major retailers and software companies—including companies that are household names—plan to enter the online market within the next six months.

The music industry's massive educational campaign

The music industry has, for a number of years, undertaken a massive campaign to educate consumers regarding the illegality of the unauthorized distribution of copyrighted music online. Recording industry leaders, along with an unprecedented coalition of other groups like the National Music Publishers' Association, the Country Music Association, the Gospel Music Association, the American Federation of Television and Radio Artists, American Federation of Musicians, ASCAP [American Society of Composers, Authors, and Publishers], BMI [Broadcast Music, Inc.], SESAC [a performing rights organization for songwriters and publishers], the Songwriters Guild of America, Nashville Songwriters Association International, National Association of Recording Merchandisers, and many others, as well as individual songwriters, recording artists, retailers, and record companies have been educating music fans that the epidemic of illegal distribution of music not only robs songwriters and recording artists of their livelihoods, but also undermines the future of music itself by depriving the industry of the resources it needs to find and develop new talent. In addition, it threatens the jobs of tens of thousands of less celebrated people in the music industry, from engineers and technicians to warehouse workers and record store clerks.

The message of this campaign has been very clear: copying or distributing copyrighted music over the Internet without permission is stealing, plain and simple. Downloading illegal copies is no different than shoplifting CDs out of a record store, and uploading those recordings for others to illegally copy is no different than handing out stolen CDs on the street corner—and the act of downloading or uploading music on peer-to-peer networks is not an anonymous one. This message has been conveyed to the public in a series of print and broadcast ads featuring more than a hundred major artists and songwriters who ask their fans to stop stealing their music. These ads have appeared in a wide variety of outlets, including USA Today, BET, and MTV. The Grammy award–winning artists participating in this campaign range from country artists Brooks & Dunn and Martina McBride to rock artist Peter Gabriel to Christian artist Steven Curtis Chapman to opera star Luciano Pavarotti to hip hop artists DMX and Missy Elliot to legends Stevie Wonder, Brian Wilson, Don Henley and Elton John, among many others. Other participants include songwriters, session musicians, and retail store owners discussing the impact of music piracy in terms of lost sales, lost jobs, and closed stores.

This antipiracy message is also featured on a music industry website, www.musicunited.org, which contains a number of clips from this educational campaign. The website also includes a wide array of pertinent information, including a description of the governing law, a list of legal online music sources, a guide for parents, as well as step-by-step instructions on how to disable or uninstall peer-to-peer software used to illegally offer music for copying.

Since April 2003, RIAA has been sending Instant Messages—and has now sent well over 4 million—directly to infringers on peer-to-peer networks. These messages inform infringers that their actions are illegal and direct them to the Music United website (www.musicunited.org) for information on how they can avoid breaking the law. While some users are responding to RIAA's messages by ceasing their illegal conduct, others have chosen to react by questioning RIAA's enforcement campaign rather than their own conduct. Kazaa, far from cooperating with this attempt to educate its users about the law, reconfigured the newest version of its software to disable the instant messaging system, thereby preventing RIAA from sending messages to Kazaa's newest users. Kazaa did not, however, change its "default" settings, which, as noted above, automatically make each user's files available for copying by others.

The Kazaa's of the world have done and will do anything within their power to facilitate copyright infringement.

Moreover, prior to filing suits, RIAA publicly announced its intent to do so, giving infringers another opportunity to discontinue their illegal conduct. Since our enforcement effort commenced, virtually every major newspaper and television news channel, and hundreds of local news outlets, has covered our efforts. One of the benefits of this heightened awareness is that millions of parents around the nation are beginning, possibly for the first time ever, to talk to their children about what they are doing online.

The Digital Millennium Copyright Act

RIAA is collecting evidence pursuant to what is commonly referred to as the information subpoena provision of the Digital Millennium Copyright Act ("DMCA"). Congress enacted the DMCA in 1998 to encourage development of the Internet's potential, while at the same time protecting against the "massive piracy" of copyrighted works that Internet technology permits. One of the purposes of the DMCA was to allow copyright holders to enforce their copyrights against direct infringers rather than the Internet Service Providers ("ISPs"). Thus, in crafting the DMCA, Congress included a fair and balanced procedure—the information subpoena provision—to ensure that copyright owners, with the help of ISPs, have an accessible and efficient mechanism for identifying individuals who are using the Internet to commit piracy.

The balance struck by Congress in [DMCA] was the result of a give and take—in the best sense—between the interests of ISPs and copyright owners, and the need to protect consumers. Congress recognized that traditional enforcement remedies available to copyright owners were insufficient in an era in which massive amounts of piracy could occur instantly at the hands of anyone with an Internet connection.

ISPs recognized that in a digital world they could have exposure to copyright claims, and thus sought from Congress limitations on liability in the DMCA. ISPs wanted copyright owners to focus on the direct infringers, but recognized that ISPs often would be the sole source for identifying individuals who are engaged in online piracy. So, in exchange for exempting ISPs from any monetary liability for the infringing activities occurring on or over their networks and connections (subject, of course, to certain prerequisites), Congress created a framework by which copyright owners, with the assistance of ISPs, could expeditiously identify individuals engaging in infringing activities online. That compromise—expeditious access for copyright owners to identifying information of infringers, in exchange for broad liability limitations for ISPs—is as fair today as it was in 1998.

It is important to note that absent the broad liability limitations of the DMCA, ISPs would most certainly be liable for secondary copyright infringement for the actions of their subscribers. ISPs who resist DMCA subpoenas are trying to enjoy the safe harbor benefit provided them by the DMCA, without shouldering the minimal corollary burden of responding to subpoenas, which is even less burdensome than would be responding to a notice to remove infringing material from their networks. That fact helps explain why Judge [John D.] Bates—the federal district judge who presided over the subpoena enforcement proceedings between RIAA and Verizon—concluded as follows: "It would not serve the public interest for Verizon to continue to receive the benefits of the [DMCA]—liability protection—without the concomitant obligations of disclosing the identity of an alleged infringer [under DMCA]."

To achieve their purpose, DMCA subpoenas must bear fruit quickly. An individual Internet pirate can cause tens of thousands of infringing copies to be distributed in a single day. In the case of recordings that have not yet been released publicly, the economic impact of this viral propagation can be devastating. Thus, as Judge Bates noted, Congress provided "express and repeated direction to make the subpoena process 'expeditious.'"

Prior to filing suits, RIAA publicly announced its intent to do so.

At the same time, Congress carefully built safeguards into [DMCA] to ensure that it is used only to enforce valid copyright claims. A copyright owner or its agent must supply a "sworn declaration to the effect that the purpose for which the subpoena is sought is to obtain the identity of an alleged infringer and that such information will only be used for the purpose of protecting rights under this title." The copyright owner must also file a notification that, among other things, identifies material being infringed and information sufficient to allow the service provider to locate the material and, if appropriate, disable access to it. By substantially complying with this notification requirement, the copyright owner or its agent has established the bona fides of its ownership and claim of infringement.

RIAA recognizes that a failure to adhere to any of these requirements is a justification for denying the subpoena and that any copyright owner who misrepresents itself in satisfying these requirements is potentially liable for damages, including attorney's fees. Thus, as described further below, RIAA takes great care to ensure that a user is illegally distributing or copying copyrighted recordings before it files a request for a subpoena.

Targeting the most serious offenders

Moreover, although the DMCA sets forth the minimum requirements for seeking a subpoena, RIAA is not seeking a subpoena as to everyone who is illegally distributing copyrighted recordings. Rather, at this time, RIAA is focusing on egregious infringers, those who are engaging in substantial amounts of illegal activity. In so prioritizing its efforts, RIAA is acting no differently than anyone in this country whose property rights have been violated and who is faced with a decision whether to press a legal claim: we are making a judgment as to whether pursuing a possible lawsuit is appropriate given the circumstances.

RIAA is focusing on egregious infringers, those who are engaging in substantial amounts of illegal activity.

As discussed above, peer-to-peer networks like FastTrack and Gnutella are, by design and practice, open networks that enable individual users to search for and copy files located on the hard-drives of other users on the network. To gather evidence against individual infringers, RIAA typically uses software that searches the public directories available to any user of a peer-to-peer network. These directories list all the files that other users of the network are currently offering to distribute. By logging onto these open networks and searching for recordings owned by RIAA's members just like any other user, the software finds users who are offering to distribute copyrighted music files. When the software finds such a user, it downloads a sample of the infringing files, along with the date and time it accessed the files, and locates the user's Internet Protocol ("IP") address. Additional information that is publicly available allows RIAA to then identify the infringer's Internet Service Provider.

Before acting on any of the information obtained by the software, an employee at RIAA manually reviews and verifies the information. And, before filing a request for a subpoena, RIAA sends the infringer's ISP advance notice that RIAA intends to issue a subpoena with respect to a particular IP address. Among other things, that allows the ISP, if it wishes, to notify its subscriber that its account is soon to be the subject of a subpoena request. Only after completing all of these steps does RIAA request a subpoena from the clerk of court (using the standard set forth in the DMCA as discussed above), seeking from the ISP identifying information for the individual whose account was being used to distribute the copyrighted music.

As demonstrated by our first-round of lawsuits, RIAA is in no way targeting "de minimis" users. RIAA is gathering evidence and preparing lawsuits only against individual computer users who are illegally distributing a substantial amount of copyrighted music. As indicated above, the subpoenas issued at the request of RIAA thus far involve infringers distributing, on average, 1000 copyrighted recordings. That said RIAA does not condone any illegal copying—and does not want anyone to think that even a little illegal activity is acceptable. Indeed, in the case of a recording that has not yet been released, the illegal distribution of just that one file can have a devastating impact on the sales of the forthcoming album.

Last spring [2003], the record companies brought suits against college students who had established and were running unauthorized peer-to-peer networks on their college networks, on which they were illegally distributing tens of thousands of recordings. The industry settled those cases for $12,500 to $17,000. While every case is unique, we intend to be similarly fair and proportionate with respect to individual infringers and to consider each individual's circumstances.

Safeguards on the information obtained about P2P users

As discussed above, the DMCA itself builds in ample safeguards for the privacy of individuals. As Judge Bates held, "These [DMCA information subpoena] protections ensure that a service provider will not be forced to disclose its customer's identifying information without a reasonable showing that there has been copyright infringement" and "these requirements provide substantial protection to service providers and their customers against overly aggressive copyright owners and unwarranted subpoenas." As Judge Bates noted in his decision, the DMCA subpoena process "provides greater threshold protection against issuance of an unsupported subpoena than is available in the context of a John Doe action." This is undoubtedly true.

Under the DMCA subpoena process, there are statutory limits on the type of information a copyright owner can obtain via subpoena and the purpose for which that information can be used. Under a DMCA subpoena, a copyright owner can only receive information that is necessary to identify and contact the alleged infringer—such as a name, address, phone number, and e-mail address. More importantly, the copyright owner is statutorily limited to using that information exclusively for purposes of enforcing its copyright. Compare that to filing a "John Doe" lawsuit, in which any aggrieved party could issue a subpoena requesting anything relating to the subscriber account, including user habits, website visits, and payment records. Moreover, once that information has been provided to a copyright owner via a subpoena in the context of a John Doe lawsuit, there are no statutory restrictions whatsoever on how it can be used or with whom it can be shared.

In short, requiring copyright owners to file John Doe lawsuits would provide fewer protections to an ISP's subscribers, while effectively depriving copyright owners of expeditious access to an alleged infringer's information. That would defeat the careful balance crafted by Congress in the DMCA. Moreover, a substantial influx of John Doe suits would be much more burdensome on the court system. If RIAA were filing John Doe lawsuits in place of each of these DMCA subpoenas, that would affect not only the clerk's office but also the judges.

RIAA shares [Congress's] concern with respect to not overwhelming the court. It thus has worked with the clerk's office, since prior to beginning our heightened efforts, to establish a process (including providing files electronically) that is acceptable to the court, and has issued its subpoenas on a rolling basis to minimize any impact on the workings of the clerk's office. Moreover, RIAA is willing—and would very much like—to reduce substantially the number of subpoenas it issues by providing multiple IP addresses for the same ISP on each subpoena. RIAA believes the DMCA allows this practice but, because many of the ISPs have objected, to date the RIAA has issued separate subpoenas for each IP address. Providing multiple addresses per subpoena would significantly reduce the administrative tasks for the clerk's office, and any support you could provide on this issue would be greatly appreciated.

Copyright infringers on peer-to-peer networks should have little expectation of privacy. Individuals on peer-to-peer networks have opened their computers, permitting access to countless others to copy whatever they wish. As Judge Bates observed, "it is hard to understand just what privacy expectation he or she has after essentially opening the computer to the world." The use of peer-to-peer networks is not anonymous: the user's IP address is publicly available to anyone else on the peer-to-peer network, and the user's ISP can determine which subscriber was using that IP address. Moreover, almost all ISPs disclose in their User's Terms of Service that, pursuant to the DMCA, they must provide the subscriber's identity to a copyright holder when there is reason to believe copyrights are being infringed. For example, Verizon informs its subscribers that it will "disclose individual customer information to an outside entity . . . when Verizon is served with valid legal process for customer information."

A fair and balanced strategy

Although there is no silver bullet solution to the growing problem of music piracy over the Internet, we believe that a three-prong approach to the problem consisting of education, legitimate alternatives, and enforcement is a fair and balanced strategy for revitalizing the music industry in the digital age.

10

The Music Industry's Lawsuits Against Online Music Sharers Are Misguided

Billboard

Billboard *is a weekly magazine of the music industry.*

The music industry's strategy of curbing online music sharing with lawsuits is futile. Illegal copying of music will continue as long as it is so easy to do, and therefore the music industry should pursue technological ways to prevent piracy. The music industry should also continue its efforts to educate consumers about the illegality of music piracy and to encourage services such as iTunes that offer legal music downloads. All three of these approaches would be more positive and engender less ill will among consumers than would lawsuits.

Pity poor Herakles. Somewhere around 2000 B.C., he noticed that his dog's mouth had been stained purple by eating snails. That gave him an idea. He used the snails to make a purple dye and used that to make a grand, purple robe.

He gave the robe to the King of Tyre as a gift, and the king was so taken by the color that he decreed that the rulers of Phoenicia should wear it as a royal symbol. Suddenly, Herakles had a very hot product on his hands, and the kingdom became renowned for its purple dye. Even Aristotle noted its preciousness in his writings, valuing it at 10 to 20 times its weight in gold.

But Tyre's monopoly was short-lived. Both the Egyptians and the ancient Jews quickly pirated the formula to produce their own royal purple and royal blue dyes. Tyre's market and sales were undercut, and Herakles faded into obscurity.

There is a lesson in this for the music industry.

Prostitution may be the oldest profession, but piracy is probably the second-oldest. If civilization has been unable to stamp out either in at least 40 centuries, it stands to reason that the Recording Industry Association of America's latest effort to eradicate music piracy is likely to suffer the same fate.

But don't try telling that to the music industry. Deeply frustrated by failed educational efforts, the RIAA now vows to get tough not only on the services that foster file sharing but also on individuals—even teens—who open their music files to others over the Internet.

Piracy is a serious problem, but lawsuits and tougher laws won't solve it.

The link between prostitution and piracy is closer than you might think. As any cop on the beat will tell you, when busting pimps and prostitutes fails, go after the johns. It doesn't work either, but it always looks good on the news.

Basically, that's the RIAA's strategy. And as 40 centuries of history prove, it will be just about as effective.

Lawsuits are not the answer

Make no mistake: Piracy is a serious problem, but lawsuits and tougher laws won't solve it. What the industry needs is a market solution. It has the essence of that now with Apple's iTunes service.

The industry needs to stay the course, keep focused on education and do everything it can to foster legal digital downloading. That includes convincing hold-out artists to make their music available.

It also needs to come up with viable encryption technology. Although it's called piracy, the problem is forgery. If the U.S. Treasury can thwart counterfeiters, the music industry should be able to do the same to protect music from being copied.

Meanwhile, law enforcement should focus on the real problem: organized crime. Domestically and particularly overseas, organized crime and possibly even terrorist groups are pirating far more music and doing more damage to the industry than little Johnny with his iMac.

We can understand the industry's frustration, but waging a legal war on average Americans will generate nothing in the end but more ill will.

11

Online File Sharing Will Benefit Society

Hal Plotkin

Hal Plotkin is a journalist based in San Francisco, California. He wrote the following viewpoint in April 2000, when the first major online music sharing service, Napster, was still in operation.

Napster and other peer-to-peer (P2P) networks are not just about sharing music. All manner of human creations—including books, movies, and paintings, as well as music—can be put into digital form, and once digitized, can be freely shared via P2P networks. P2P networks will therefore revolutionize the way that people obtain access to these works. Instead of everyone buying a particular book, for example, most people will be able to access the book's content for free. People who currently sell creative works will have to find new ways of profiting from their creations—musicians would still be able to sell concert tickets, for example, and authors could still charge for physical copies of books (though their content would be free online). The revolution in sharing will be painful for many, but ultimately society will benefit once everyone has free and easy access to creative works.

It's hard to overstate the significance of the rise of Napster. Some say it's just another expression of human greed, a manifestation of the desire to get something for nothing.

But the seemingly inconsequential act of trading music online may eventually come to be seen in a much more positive light; as a critical turning point when consumers, and not just open-source programmers, began using the Internet to breathe new life into the human instinct for community and for helping one another.

But before we get to the larger implications, let's first explain how Napster works.

Once installed, the free Napster software gives users access to the MP3 music files on the hard drives of any other online members of the Napster community. In return, Napster users are expected, but not required, to give other Napster users access to any MP3 files on their hard drives.

Hal Plotkin, "Napsterizing: How Free Music Will Change the Planet," *San Francisco Chronicle*, April 6, 2000. Copyright © 2000 by the *San Francisco Chronicle*. Reproduced by permission of the author.

There are currently more than 500,000 songs available within the Napster music community, which usually has hundreds of linked participating computers.

And remember, we're talking about a phenomenon that is just a few months old [in 2000]. The number of available songs is sure to grow.

Ethical concerns

There are some serious ethical and legal concerns about Napsterism.

A few popular MP3s are being distributed with the permission of their creators. But the vast majority of the digital tunes now available through Napster are pirated, high-quality commercial recordings of everyone from Frank Sinatra to Erykah Badu.

The dimensions of the ethical problems involved hit me particularly hard while I was downloading a favorite Bob Dylan song. . . .

Others are free to disagree, but I know I'm not alone when I confess to loving, even revering Bob Dylan. The thought of ripping him off, of taking his art without paying for it, seems a karmic hazard of the highest order.

Midway through the download, I clicked the mouse button to cancel. Then I thought it over.

I'm not sure yet whether my thinking process represents good solid reasoning or just opportunistic rationalizing, but I eventually came to the conclusion downloading Dylan's tune didn't constitute theft. At least, not for me.

After all, I had paid Dylan and his record company for that particular tune on at least four prior occasions. Back in the early seventies, I bought the song on a vinyl LP. A few years later, I purchased the same song on an obsolescence-bound eight-track tape. In the early eighties, I paid even more for it on cassette and finally, just a few years ago, anted up again for a re-released CD.

I figured Dylan would be fine with a freebie for my fifth purchase. Sort of like a frequent-buyer discount.

While that may—or may not—have resolved my personal ethical dilemma about that one particular song and artist, it does nothing at all to address the larger issues.

What about people who have never paid a dime for the songs they download? How can the recording industry, and the artists it supports, survive if it's no longer necessary for people to purchase recordings in order to own them?

A new, sharing world

That's the new world we're entering.

The lesson of Napsterism is that anything that can be digitized will be digitized; and that once something is digitized it can, and inevitably will, be freely shared over the Internet.

We're not just talking about music here.

We're also talking about all other human creations that can be digitized: paintings, photos, books, movies, and poetry, to name a few, as well as virtually all forms of human knowledge, from cooking recipes to computer programming lessons to brain chemistry archives.

Ironically, just a decade after it seemed the Cold War had finally ended the often-bloody argument between capitalists and communists, the technology behind Napster is helping to re-divide the world along similar philosophical lines.

On the one hand, you have the old-line capitalists, the survival-of-the-fittest crowd, who take their lessons from Charles Darwin. For them, it's a dog-eat-dog world where the main goal is to make sure your dog wins.

And then you have a much smaller band of communitarians who, knowingly or not, take their cues from the perceptive but lesser-known Russian philosopher, Peter Kropotkin, who made his name taking on Darwinism.

Kropotkin maintained that the tendency toward what he called "mutual aid," the desire to be of voluntary service to one another, represents the highest, most-advanced stage of evolution. Ants have prospered as a species, Kropotkin would argue, due to their innate sense of community, not because they are individually able to slash one another's throats.

Darwin's followers had the edge for most of the last century, which culminated as it did in the fall of the Soviet bloc, an experience that proved Kropotkin's vision could not be imposed by government fiat.

The lesson of Napsterism is that . . . once something is digitized it can, and inevitably will, be freely shared over the Internet.

But the rise of Napsterism may prove that Kropotkin didn't have it all wrong.

The open-source computer programming movement was an early form of Napsterism. And, most likely, there are many more to come. Just imagine the possibilities.

The advent of cheap canvas-like flat panel displays, for example, means it might be possible to have a digital Renoir on our wall one night, and a Picasso the next. Although it sounds like a telecom commercial, every song, drama, movie, all works ever recorded will be available on someone's computer somewhere, which means that should they choose to share, it will be available to everyone everywhere.

Breaking an embargo on any form of digital goods will require just one person willing to share that item online.

We might, for example, see similar Napster-like communities centered on other activities. Cooking recipes, for example, could be freely exchanged through a culinary community that links hard drives together; child-rearing strategies, resources and ideas, through a parenting community.

Whether it's architecture, computer skills, plumbing techniques, or dress-making patterns, virtually every facet of life might well be touched by the growing momentum of Napster-like sharing communities.

Sharing communities feed on themselves. More resources become available as more people join. As more resources become available, even more people join. Those who don't participate, on the other hand, find themselves isolated by the very selfishness they thought would be their protection.

The genie is out of the bottle

The advent of sharing communities does, however, pose a significant set of problems for those who used to sell whatever items are being shared. Like it or not, they're going to have to find new ways to support their creative processes.

Take recording artists, for example.

Although the recording industry is trying, it's far too late to put the MP3 genie back in the bottle. Record industry execs currently hope to figure out some nifty technical fix. They're banking on more powerful encryption technologies, digital watermarking services, or a similar solution to the problem of pirated digital recordings.

The underlying enabling technology now being used to trade music files makes the rise of . . . new sharing communities all but certain.

But there will be no fix. At least, no lasting fix.

Any digital file that can be played on one device can be captured and recorded in its exact original form by some other device. Period. End of story.

What's more, any file that can be encrypted can eventually be decrypted. After all, both sides have access to the same computing power.

For recording artists, this means they probably won't be able to count on making most of their money through sales of their recordings in the years ahead. One can argue whether that's fair or not, or whether it's a good or bad thing. Either way, though, it's inevitable.

The only alternative is to give some authority the right to inspect and approve every single digital transmission sent and received, a level of intrusion into our lives that most would find intolerable were it even possible, which it is not.

That doesn't mean recording artists are destined to go broke. But recording artists, like others who sell digital goods, will have to find new, more creative ways to generate income.

Fortunately, there's reason to hope wider distribution of free music will make good artists more popular than ever. The best of them might even get smart and start charging what the market will bear when they make live appearances.

That could mean higher average ticket prices. But that seems a fair trade-off for free recordings. In the old days, record sales were the music industry's dog and live concerts the marketing tail. In the future, we'll be looking at an entirely different animal.

Recording artists might, for example, offer preferred ticket deals to fans who buy subscriptions, sell advertising on websites where they distribute the complete collection of their own MP3s, or provide more personalized services, such as custom-made or even autographed CDs and posters.

Many younger artists have already embraced the MP3 format. They realize it represents something long dreamed of, a way to get music in front of the masses without having to cut a deal with industry gatekeepers first.

More established acts may see this as an unwelcome development, but recordings of all kinds will eventually become loss-leaders, similar to the below-cost sale items that lead consumers into a store so they can be sold something else.

It's possible at least some artists will fare even better in the long run as they find new ways to generate cash from an even larger community of fans.

A positive transformation

In the meantime, Napster-like sharing communities will soon begin to transform many other areas of our social and economic life. The underlying enabling technology now being used to trade music files makes the rise of these new sharing communities all but certain.

We'll all lead richer lives the more people share what they have or know.

Peter Kropotkin wouldn't have been a bit surprised.

Organizations and Websites

The editors have compiled the following list of organizations concerned with the issues debated in this book. The descriptions are derived from materials provided by the organizations. All have publications or information available for interested readers. The list was compiled on the date of publication of the present volume; the information provided here may change. Be aware that many organizations take several weeks or longer to respond to inquiries, so allow as much time as possible.

American Society of Composers, Authors, and Publishers (ASCAP)
One Lincoln Plaza, New York, NY 10023
(212) 621-6000
website: www.ascap.com

ASCAP is a membership association of over 170,000 U.S. composers, songwriters, lyricists, and music publishers. ASCAP protects the rights of its members by licensing and distributing royalties for public performances of their copyrighted works. ASCAP opposes illegal file sharing, and congressional testimony of several ASCAP members on the subject of Internet copyright issues is available on the organization's website. The organization publishes *Playback* magazine.

Berkman Center for Internet and Society
Harvard Law School, Baker House
1587 Massachusetts Ave., Cambridge, MA 02138
(617) 495-7547
website: http://cyber.law.harvard.edu

The Berkman Center is a research program founded to explore cyberspace, share in its study, and help pioneer its development. Intellectual property issues on the Internet are among the program's main topics of interest. The program's website offers a wealth of papers and news stories on Internet piracy and copyright issues.

Canadian Value of Music Coalition (CVOMC)
890 Yonge St., 12th Floor, Toronto, ON M4W 3P4 Canada
website: www.keepmusiccoming.com

The coalition is a public awareness and education campaign designed to influence Canadians' attitudes toward recorded music. CVOMC advocates the idea that when people buy music, they help artists create more music and allow new artists a chance to be heard. The coalition's website offers information on music issues, a message board where visitors can express their views, and public service announcements that users can watch online.

Center for the Public Domain
3937 St. Marks Rd., Durham, NC 27707
(919) 549-8388
website: www.centerpd.org

The center is a philanthropic foundation dedicated to preserving a strong, robust public domain in which the public has access to a rich diversity of ideas and creative works. It opposes draconian copyright laws and efforts to privatize and commercialize information. Through grant making, original research, conferences, and collaborative programs, the center seeks to call attention to the importance of the public domain. The center's website contains overviews and papers on issues related to intellectual property, copyright law, and patent law.

Downhill Battle
e-mail: contact@downhillbattle.org • website: www.downhillbattle.org

Downhill Battle is a nonprofit campaign that believes that digital music has the potential to give rise to a system in which artists are better compensated for their work. Downhill Battle supports a boycott of the Recording Industry Association of America because of its lawsuits against online music sharers and its members' business practices, which Downhill Battle argues are unscrupulous and prevent independent musicians from being heard. The Downhill Battle website contains numerous articles on new developments in the controversy over online music sharing.

Electronic Frontier Foundation (EFF)
454 Shotwell St., San Francisco, CA 94110
(415) 436-9333
website: www.eff.org

EFF is an advocacy organization that works to defend civil liberties and individual rights, primarily in cases where legal and technological issues intersect. EFF believes that peer-to-peer networks have enormous potential, but that the music industry, in its zeal to stop illegal trading of copyrighted songs online, will cause significant damage to the developers of this technology. The foundation has provided legal representation to online music sharers and the developers of peer-to-peer networks. Through its "Let the Music Play" campaign, the foundation opposes the recording industry's crackdown on online music sharing and believes that the government should explore ways of making online file sharing legal while still compensating artists. More information is available at the EFF website.

International Federation of the Phonographic Industry (IFPI)
IFPI Secretariat, 54 Regent St., London, W1B 5RE United Kingdom
website: www.ifpi.org

IFPI is the organization representing the international recording industry. It comprises a membership of fifteen hundred record producers and distributors in seventy-six countries. One of the federation's top priorities is fighting piracy, and to this end it conducts research on piracy, advises its members on legal and technological strategies to combat piracy, and lobbies governments to enforce copyright laws. IFPI publishes an annual report on music piracy as well as a quarterly newsletter.

International Intellectual Property Alliance (IIPA)
1747 Pennsylvania Ave. NW, Suite 825, Washington, DC 20006-4637
(202) 833-4198
website: www.iipa.com

IIPA is a private sector coalition formed to represent U.S. copyright-based industries in worldwide efforts to improve international protection of copyrighted materials. IIPA's goal is a legal and enforcement regime for copyright that not only deters piracy, but also fosters technological and cultural development in other countries, and encourages local investment and employment. The IIPA website offers country-by-country reports and statistics on piracy.

Music United for Strong Internet Copyright (MUSIC)
e-mail: info@musicunited.org • website: www.musicunited.org

Music United for Strong Internet Copyright is a coalition of more than twenty trade organizations within the music industry. Its mission is to promote public awareness of the legal and moral issues surrounding online music sharing. The MUSIC website contains information on what types of activities, including CD copying and online file sharing, violate copyright laws.

National Association of Recording Merchandisers (NARM)
9 Eves Dr., Suite 120, Marlton, NJ 08053
(856) 596-2221
website: www.narm.com

NARM is a trade association representing nearly one thousand music retailers, wholesalers, and distributors. NARM believes that online music sharing is illegal and a serious threat to the music industry. Many NARM member companies are also part of the Recording Industry Association of America, which in September 2003 began filing lawsuits against individuals who make files containing copyrighted songs available for online download by others. The NARM website offers a variety of position papers, member testimony, and other resources on Internet piracy.

P2P United
Adam Eisgrau, Executive Director, c/o Flanagan Consulting LLC
1317 F St. NW, Suite 800, Washington, DC 20004
website: www.p2punited.org

P2P United is the unified voice of the peer-to-peer technology industry's leading companies and proponents. P2P United represents and champions the P2P industry and technology to policy makers, opinion leaders, the media, and the public. The organization does not support Internet piracy, and disputes the idea that Internet file sharing is mainly a tool for illegal copying. The organization's website offers issue overviews and news updates on legal and technological developments in the P2P field.

Public Knowledge
1875 Connecticut Ave. NW, Suite 650, Washington, DC 20009
(202) 518-0020
website: www.publicknowledge.org

Public Knowledge is a public-interest advocacy organization dedicated to fortifying and defending a vibrant information commons. The group works with libraries, educators, scientists, artists, musicians, journalists, consumers, software programmers, civic groups, and enlightened businesses to oppose excessive copyright laws and preserve a free and open Internet. Public Knowledge opposes the record industry's efforts to stamp out online music sharing. The organization's website offers information on relevant court cases, pending legislation, and events related to these issues.

Recording Industry Association of America (RIAA)
website: www.riaa.com

RIAA is the trade group that represents the U.S. recording industry. Its mission is to foster a business and legal climate that supports and promotes its members' creative and financial vitality. RIAA has led the music industry's fight against online music sharing, lobbying Congress, educating the public, and pursuing legal action against peer-to-peer networks and the people who use them in its efforts to curb Internet piracy. The RIAA website offers information on its antipiracy efforts as well as on music sales and copyright issues.

Websites

Bricklin.com
website: www.Bricklin.com

This is the personal website of software developer Dan Bricklin. It offers numerous essays that Bricklin has written on online file sharing and its effect on the music industry, including "The Recording Industry Is Trying to Kill the Goose That Lays the Golden Egg" and "How Will the Artists Get Paid?"

InfoAnarchy
website: www.infoanarchy.org

The creators of this site believe that Internet technology has made the copyright laws of the past unenforceable, and warn that the entertainment industry's efforts to enforce copyright on the Internet are restricting freedom of speech and the free flow of information online. The site offers information on peer-to-peer networks and other technologies that can be used to help fight restrictions on the Internet.

International Music Industry Reform Association (IMIRA)
website: www.imira.org

IMIRA's members believe that more meaningful dialogue, rather than prosecutions or an information revolution, is needed to address online copyright issues.

p2pnet
website: www.p2pnet.net

This website provides news, commentary, and resources on Internet file sharing.

Pro-Music
website: www.pro-music.org

This site is part of the music industry's campaign to raise awareness about the illegality and harm of Internet piracy. It provides information on the copyright laws as well as numerous links to sites that sell digital music legally.

Bibliography

Books

John Alderman
Sonic Boom: Napster, MP3, and the New Pioneers of Music. Cambridge, MA: Perseus, 2001.

Bruce Haring
Beyond the Charts: MP3 and the Digital Music Revolution. Los Angeles: JM Northern Media, 2000.

Lawrence Lessig
The Future of Ideas: The Fate of the Commons in a Connected World. New York: Random House, 2001.

Jessica Litman
Digital Copyright: Protecting Intellectual Property on the Internet. Amherst, NY: Prometheus Books, 2001.

Trevor Merriden
Irresistible Forces: The Business Legacy of Napster and the Growth of the Underground Internet. Oxford, UK: Capstone, 2001.

Siva Vaidhyanathan
Copyrights and Copywrongs: The Rise of Intellectual Property and How It Threatens Creativity. New York: New York University Press, 2001.

Periodicals

Alex Adrianson
"Stopping Music Piracy Without Breaking the Internet," *Consumer's Research Magazine,* October 2003.

Paul Boutin
"Don't Steal Music, Pretty Please," *Salon.com,* December 18, 2001.

Sam Brownback
"Who Will Police the Pirate-Hunters?" *Wall Street Journal,* October 7, 2003.

Business Week
"Hollywood Heist: Will Tinseltown Let Techies Steal the Show?" July 14, 2003.

Damien Cave
"Chained Melodies," *Salon.com,* March 13, 2002.

Economist
"A Fine Balance," January 15, 2003.

Economist
"Tipping Hollywood the Black Spot; Piracy and the Movie Business," August 30, 2003.

Economist
"Upbeat: Is the Threat of Online Piracy Receding?" November 1, 2003.

Mike France
"Striking Back; How the Music Industry Charted Its Crusade Against Web Pirates," *Business Week,* September 29, 2003.

Nick Gillespie
"Shut Up 'n' Play Yer Guitar," *Reason,* September 15, 2003.

Gloria Goodale	"Don't Call Me a Pirate. I'm an Online Fan," *Christian Science Monitor*, July 18, 2003.
Lev Grossman	"It's All Free! Music! Movies! TV Shows! Millions of People Download Them Everyday. Is Digital Piracy Killing the Entertainment Industry?" *Time*, May 5, 2003.
Carl S. Kaplan	"Curbing Peer-to-Peer Piracy," *Technology Review*, May 2003.
Terrell Kenneth and Seth Rosen	"A Nation of Pirates," *U.S. News & World Report*, July 14, 2003.
Steven Levy	"The Noisy War over Napster," *Newsweek*, June 5, 2000.
Charles C. Mann	"Heavenly Jukebox," *Atlantic Monthly*, September 2000.
Johnnie L. Roberts	"Out of Tune: Picking on Little Kids and Old Ladies? What Were the Record Companies Thinking? They Say It's Life or Death," *Newsweek*, September 22, 2003.
Cary Sherman	"File Sharing Is Illegal. Period," *USA Today*, September 19, 2003.
John Snyder and Ben Snyder	"Embrace File-Sharing or Die," *Salon.com*, February 1, 2003.
Chris Taylor	"Burn, Baby, Burn," *Time*, May 20, 2002.
Time	"A Crisis of Content: It's Not Just Pop Music. Every Industry That Trades in Intellectual Property—from Publishing to Needlework Patterns—Could Get Napsterized," October 2, 2000.
Cynthia L. Webb	"RIAA vs. the People," *Washington Post*, September 9, 2003.

Index